Written by Joyce Hamman
Edited by Linda Milliken
Design by Wendy Loreen
Illustration by Priscilla Burris
Cover Illustration by Priscilla Burris

About the Author

Joyce Hamman has over 16 years experience working with early childhood developmental programs. She is a frequent speaker for the National Association for the Education of Young Children. Joyce currently educates kindergartners at the American School of the Hague, Netherlands.

ISBN 1-56472-015-2

TABLE OF CONTENTS

Teacher's Guide

Activity Guide

Resources

Theme Days

TEACHER'S GUIDE

About the Book

- You are provided with plans, material lists and activities for 20 days of thematic learning.
- There are activity suggestions for opening and closing the day as well as those that build fundamental readiness skills, motor development and critical thinking. There are also literature links, snack suggestions and rhymes and chants for resting and remembering.

Planning Tips

- Plan a year-long schedule of theme days. Decide how many per year or per month you would like to have. Then select the days by reviewing the Table of Contents and the theme-day activities themselves.
- When you have selected the theme days, read through the suggested activities again. The activities, in most cases, may be incorporated in any order into a day's plans. Choose activities that fit into the time you have available and skill on which you want to focus. Not all activities need to take place in order to have a successful theme day.
- If time is limited, the activities may be extended over two days.

Preparation

- Make a list of all materials you want parents to help supply. Two weeks before the theme day, add your "needs" to the parent letter page, photocopy and send the top half home with students.
- Send home the bottom reminder portion the day before the planned theme day.
- Gather together all other required materials as listed on the first page of each theme unit. Read the activities for suggested literature and music titles. Refer to the Resource lists for additional program aids.

Theme Day Activity Objectives

Opening: Start the day with an activity that introduces the theme for the day and involves the entire class.

Literature Corner: Look here for literature titles that connect with the theme. Several are suggested, along with a short summary, to make your choice one that fits your likes and needs.

Skill Builder: These activities reinforce and develop basic readiness skills from counting and color recognition, to auditory memory and directionality.

Art Corner: Art activity correlates with the theme and provides additional opportunity to develop small motor skills as well as creative expression.

Snack Time: More than a snack! Learning is extended through associated activity.

Ready To Rest: Rhymes and chants are provided to ease children into a rest time. If older participants do not require a rest period, the chants and rhymes can still be incorporated into other parts of the day.

Music: Refer to Resources, page 7, for a listing of records and tapes to have on hand for program integration. Specific titles and sources are suggested within each theme unit.

Science: Activities provide an opportunity for students to test, observe, explore and discover.

Motor Development: Build large muscle skills with these games and movement activities.

Closing: End the day by reinforcing a concept learned during the day's activities.

Resources: Look on pages 6-7 for books, equipment, and records to supplement your program.

RESOURCES

Equipment

This equipment is incorporated into Theme Day activities.

- Chinese Jump Ropes
- Jump Ropes
- Large Plastic Hoops•
- Playground Balls
- Parachute
- Coordination Ladder
- Balance Beam
- Jump Box
- Geometric Shapes
- Scooter Boards
- Rebound Nets

Active Learning for Threes, Addison-Wesley

Circle Time Activities for Young Children, **by Deva Brashears,** Circle Time Publishing

Creativity in Early Childhood Classrooms, **by Tegano, Moran, Sawyers,** National Education Association Publication, 1991

Easy Games for Early Learners, **by Wendy Loreen,** Edupress, 1993

Games, Giggles, and Giants Steps, **by Susan Miller,** Instructor Books

The Joy of Movement in Early Childhood, **by Dr. Sandra Curtis,** Teachers College Press

Make It Today For Pre-K Play, **by Joyce Hamman,** Edupress,1993

Musical Games, Fingerplay and Rhythmic Activities for Early Childhood, **by Marian Wirth,** Parker Publishing Company

The Outside Play and Learning Book, **by Karen Miller,** *Gryphon House*

Perceptual-Motor Lesson Plans, Level-1 **by Jack Capon,** Front Row, 1975

Skills for Preschool Teachers, **by Janice J. Beaty,** Merrill Publishing

Super Book of Arts and Crafts, **by Kastoff, Gant, Milliken,** Edupress, 1993

Music

Bean Bag Activities and Coordination Skills, **Georgiana Liccione Stewart,** KIM 7055

Easy Does It, **Hap Palmer,** AR 581

Feelin' Free, **Hap Palmer,** AR 517

Finger Plays and Foot Plays for Fun and Learning, **Rosemary Hallum, Ph.D. and Henry "Buzz" Glass,** AR 618

*Holiday Piggyback Songs**,* **Warren Publishing House,** ISBN 0-911019-18-9

Heel, Toe, Away We Go!, **Georgiana Liccione Stewart,** KIM 7050

Kids' Circus, **Georgiana Liccione Stewart,** KIM 7032

Kids in Motion, **Greg and Steve, Youngheart Records,** CTP 008

Learning Basic Skills Through Music, **Hap Palmer**

Volume 1, AR 514, *Volume 2*, AR 522, *Volume 3,* AR 592

Learning Basic Skills Through Vocabulary, **Hap Palmer,** AR 521

Learning Through Movement and Song, Volume 1, **Sheri Senter,** National Pediatric Support Services

Learning with Circles and Sticks, **Hap Palmer,** AR 585

Me and My Bean Bag, **The Learning Station,** KIM 9111

Mod Marchers, **Hap Palmer,** AR 527

*More Piggyback Songs**,* **Totline Press,** ISBN 0-911019-1-02-2

Movin', **Hap Palmer,** AR 546

Preschool Favorites, **Georgiana Liccione Stewart,** KIM 9122

Quiet Moments With Greg and Steve, **Youngheart Records,** CTP 006

Restful Music for Quiet Times, **Kimbo,** KIM 9109

Rhythms on Parade, **Hap Palmer,** AR 633

Shapes in Action, **Georgiana Liccione Stewart,** KIM 7031

Singable Songs for the Very Young, **Raffi**, KSR 8102

We All Live Together, **Greg and Steve, Youngheart Records,** CTP 002

*** Indicates Songbook**

Plump Up Pillows For A Day Of Learning Fun!

GETTING READY:

5 Days before Pillow Day, send out the parent information notice provided. One day prior to the event, send home the reminder notice.

You will need these materials for Pillow Day Play *Activities:*

Opening:
- A few extra pillows for children who don't have one.

Literature Corner and Music:
- See suggested selections.

Art Corner:
- White paint • Drinking straws
- Blue construction paper
- Sponge pieces
- Cotton Balls • Glitter

Snack Time:
- Paper plates
- Plastic forks
- Napkins
- Canned ravioli
- Hot plate
- Pan
- Large spoon

Skill Builder:
- Number Cards

PILLOW DAY PLAY

We are planning a special theme day. Please read the information below and gather all the requested items to send with your child on the date indicated below.

Date:____________________

Please send: A labeled pillow that your child can play with.
Other needs:

A reminder will be sent home on the day prior to the special event.

If you would be willing to help, please sign and return this form with your child.________________

PILLOW DAY PLAY

Reminder

Tomorrow is our special Pillow Day. **Please remember to send** a labeled pillow that your child can play with and any other materials requested on our original notice. If you have any questions, please feel free to call me at_____________.

And remember to ask your child to share the learning fun they had on Pillow Day!

Sincerely,

PILLOW DAY PLAY

THE DAY'S ACTIVITIES

Form a large friendship circle. Hug your pillow then hug a friend. Share the pillow you brought. Do you know what color it is? What room in your house was it in?

Literature Corner

Bring your pillow and rest your head during story time. Suggested reading:

Nimby Cloud Book **by Jasper Tomkins,** Simon & Schuster, 1982.
Introduction to the different kinds of clouds.

It Looks Like Spilt Milk **by George Shaw,** Harper & Row, 1947
Child imagines the different shapes seen in clouds.

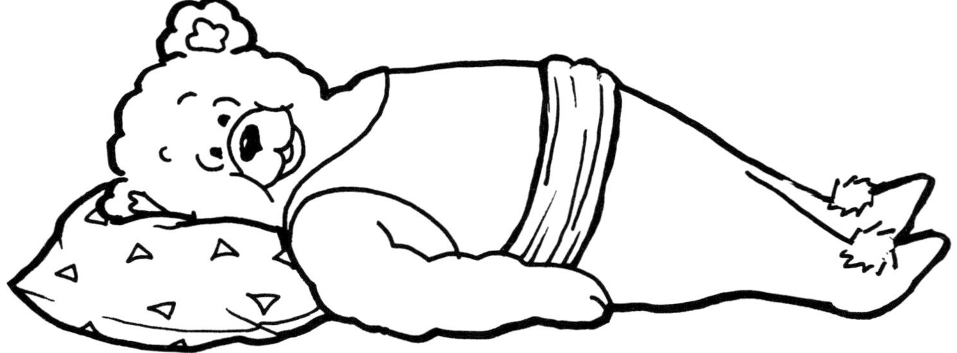

Skill Builder: Shapes & Directionality

Pillow Shapes

"Let's all put our pillows in the shape of a circle."
"Let's all stand inside the big circle shape."

"Now let's put our pillows in the shape of a square."
"Let's stand outside the square."

"Put your pillow on the floor. Stand beside it. Stand in front of it."
"Pick up your pillow. Stand under it. Now hold it as high as you can."

Art Corner

You'll need:

- *white paint*
- *sponge pieces*
- *glitter*
- *blue construction paper*
- *cotton balls*
- *drinking straws*

Sponge paint or use a straw to blow fluffy, white "pillow-shaped" clouds on blue construction paper. Spread white cotton balls or sprinkle silver glitter (or both) on the wet paint.

Snack Time

Heat and eat ravioli "pillows". Talk about their shape. Imagine what might be hidden inside. Introduce the word "pasta".

You'll Need:

- *paper plates*
- *plastic forks*
- *napkins*
- *canned ravioli*
- *hot plate*
- *pan*
- *large spoon*

Ready to Rest

Hold onto your pillow and say this little rhyme:

"Here's a friend to take to bed.
It's soft and fluffy too.
Say goodnight to your new friend
Then lie and rest your head."

PILLOW DAY PLAY

Motor Development

- Toss the pillow to a target such as a masking tape outline of a circle or a large tub.
- Space pillows around the room. Jump, crawl, hop, or think of another way to move from pillow to pillow.

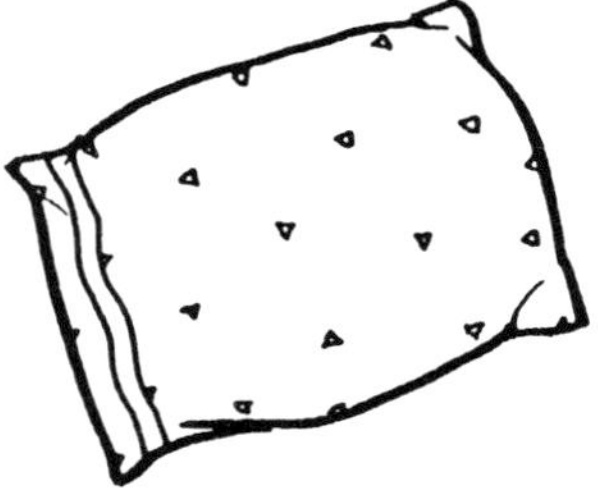

Music

Relax with your head on your pillow and listen to *Spaghetti Test* from the record ***Learning Through Movement and Song*** by Sheri Senter. (See Resources, page 7)

If that record is not available, select a quiet song for some "dreamy" listening.

Skill Builder: Body Awareness

Partner Play

Play with a partner to hold a pillow
...with your hand and their hand
...with your foot and their foot
...with your nose and their nose
...with your elbow and theirs.

Individual Play

"Put your elbow on your pillow."
"Put your forehead on your pillow."
"Rest the palm of your hand on your pillow."

Oral Language

Use a variety of body position words and ask children to follow through with the action. Show them (or ask a child to demonstrate) the action if they are unsure.

"Kneel on your pillow."

"Sit cross-legged on your pillow."

"Squat on your pillow."

"Straddle your pillow."

Skill Builder: Counting

You'll need: number cards

Invite students, by name, to put their pillow in a pile. Together, count the pillows in the pile. Return the pillows to their owner and start another pile with a different number of pillows.

Reinforce number recognition by showing the students number cards. Ask a child to find a number card that matches the number of pillows you counted in a pile.

Closing

Gather all the pillows and put them in a big pile in the center of the room. Invite each child to perform an action around the pillow pile, find his or her pillow and be dismissed for the day.

"Jason, skip, skip, skip around the pillow pile. Find yours and say goodbye."

Let Learning Go To Your Head On Hat Day!

GETTING READY:

5 Days before Hat Day, send out the parent information notice provided. One day prior to the event, send home the reminder notice.

You will need these materials for Hat Day Play *Activities:*

Opening:
- Extra hats for children who didn't bring one.

Literature Corner and Music:
- Book: See suggested titles

Art Corner:
- Fingerpaint
- Newspaper

Snack Time:
- Paper plates
- Napkins
- Frosting
- Cookies
- Raisins
- Chef's hat
- Plastic knives
- Sprinkles
- Candies

Skill Builders:
- Hats related to occupations

Motor Development:
- Parachute or large sheet
- Bean bags

HAT DAY PLAY

We are planning a special theme day. Please read the information below and gather all the requested items to send with your child on the date indicated below.

Date:_______________________

Please send: A labeled hat that your child can play with.
Other needs:

A reminder will be sent home on the day prior to the special event.

If you would be willing to help, please sign and return this form with your child._________________

HAT DAY PLAY

Reminder

Tomorrow is our special Hat Day. **Please remember to send** a labeled hat with your child and any other materials requested on our original notice. If you have any questions, please feel free to call me at

________________.

And remember to ask your child to share the learning fun they had on Hat Day!

Sincerely,

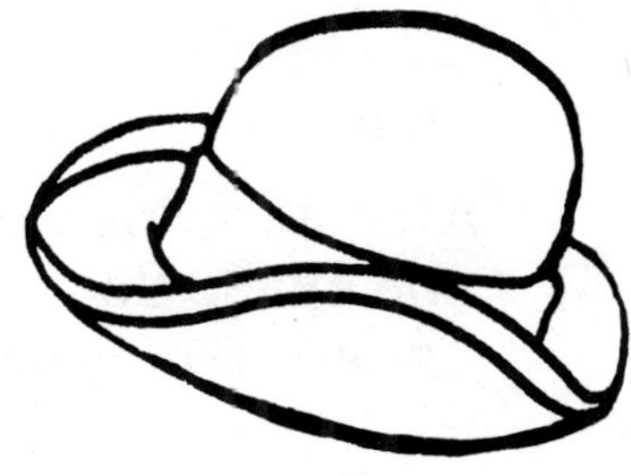

THE DAY'S ACTIVITIES

Wear your hat during opening activities. Talk about the colors and different kinds you see.

Put on some marching music and have a hat parade around the room.

Literature Corner

Wear your hat to story time. Suggested reading:

Hats, Hats, Hats **by Ann Morris**, Lothrop, Lee & Shepard Books ,1989
A hat collector meets and weds Isabel—who loves his hats.

Martin's Hats by William Morrow & Company, 1984
Martin has many exciting adventures in a variety of hats.

Caps for Sale **by Esphyr Slobodkina,** Addison-Wesley 1968
Monkeys try on hats in a hat fashion show.

Skill Builder: Memory Development

Select three children to wear their hat and sit in front of the group. Ask those in the group to look carefully at the hat each child is wearing.

After allowing examination time, take off the three hats and mix them up on the floor in front of the seated students. Invite a child from the group to replace each hat on the owner's head.

Art Corner

Make a triangle hat to wear.
You'll need:

- *one-half newspaper page*
- *fingerpaint*

Fold newspaper in half, lengthwise. Place fold on top and opening on the bottom. Fold the paper in half across the width. Open. Bring upper two corners to the middle fold line just made. The newspaper should look like a triangle on top. Fold the excess paper from the open end on both sides to make a perfect triangle. Fingerpaint the hats the color and design of choice.

Snack Time

Become pastry chefs and decorate some cookies. If possible, buy a chef's hat from a restaurant supply or borrow one from a local restaurant. Take turns wearing the hat and being the "chef in charge".

You'll Need:

- *plain sugar cookies, one for each child*
- *napkins*
- *plastic knives*
- *frosting*
- *decorating sprinkles, raisins & candies*
- *chef's hat*

Game Time

Play "Pass the Hat".

Sit in a large circle. Hold your hat in your left hand. Play music and pass the hats clockwise. Stop the music. Put the hat you are holding on your head. Take time to look at everyone in their new hats. Start the music. Take the hat off and pass it again until the music stops.

HAT DAY PLAY

Motor Development

Put all the hats under a parachute or large sheet. When a child's name is called he or she alligator crawls under the parachute, finds a hat, puts it on his or her head and crawls back out with it.

Once out from under the parachute or sheet, the child rejoins the circle and continues to hold the parachute until all classmates have had a turn. The children holding the parachute make "ripples and waves" trying to trap the alligator underneath.

Ready to Rest

Collect all the hats. Hold one up and say this rhyme:

"Whose hat is that?
Does it belong to you?
Come here and get it
Then take a rest too!

Owner retrieves his or her hat then goes to their mat to rest.

Skill Builder: Auditory Memory

Children perform each action after listening to the instructions. String two to three instructions together to develop memory.

"Put your hat on your head."

"Put your hat on your right foot then on your other foot."

"Rest your hat on your tummy, then on your knee and count to three."

Community Awareness

Collect job-related hats to share with children. Helmets, ski caps, baseball caps, hard hats, fireman hat, uniform hats or caps all lead to discussion regarding the kind of job the wearer does.

Allow the children some time to try one the different hats and pretend they are working in that profession.

Motor Development

You'll need: bean bags

Set the hats upside-down a short distance away from each child. Provide them with a bean bag. Try to toss the bean bag into the hat.

Increase the distance of the hat from the body as skill and accuracy improve.

Closing

Repeat the opening hat parade. Start the music again. Children join in the parade as they hear a description that fits their hat, until everyone is marching. Then march right out the door!

"March along with us if your hat is blue."

An Apple A Day Brings Learning Your Way!

GETTING READY:

5 Days before Apple Day, send out the parent information notice provided. One day prior to the event, send home the reminder notice.

You will need these materials for Apple Day Play *Activities:*

Opening :
- Extra apples

Art Corner:
- Red, yellow & green tempera paint
- White construction paper
- Apples

Snack Time:
- Apples
- Cinnamon
- Cutting Board
- Potato Masher
- Small bowls
- Electric skillet
- Plastic knives
- Large bowl

Motor Development
- Red, yellow & green foam balls
- Parachute or large sheet

Literature Corner & Music:
- See suggested selections

Skill Builders:
- Crayons
- Paper apples

Science
- Potting soil
- Apple seeds
- Planting container

APPLE DAY PLAY

We are planning a special theme day. Please read the information below and gather all the requested items to send with your child on the date indicated below.

Date:____________________

Please send: One apple, any color, in a paper bag

Other needs:

A reminder will be sent home on the day prior to the special event.

If you would be willing to help, please sign and return this form with your child.______________

APPLE DAY PLAY

Reminder

Tomorrow is our special Apple Day. **Please remember to send** one apple, any color, in a paper bag with your child and any other materials requested on our original notice. If you have any questions, please feel free to call me at

____________________.

And remember to ask your child to share the learning fun they had on Apple Day!

Sincerely,

APPLE DAY PLAY

THE DAY'S ACTIVITIES

Opening

Ask each child to bring an apple to school in a small paper bag. One at a time, each child gives a clue as to the color of their apple. For example, "My apple is the same color as a tomato." Once the color has been guessed, take the apple out of the bag and set it on the table for all to see.

Literature Corner

The Seasons of Arnold's Apple Tree **by Gail Gibbons,** Harcourt Brace Jovanovich 1984
A boy observes the changes of an apple tree during the four seasons.

Apple Tree **by Barrie Watts**, Silver Burdett Press 1986
Easy-to-understand text and sequential photographs of an apple's growth.

Skill Builder: Sorting & Size Comparison

Gather around the table on which the apples shared during opening were set. Count all the apples then sort them into groups by color. Finally, place all the apples in a line, working left to right, from smallest to largest.

Art Corner

You'll need:

- *red, green and yellow tempera paint*
- *white construction paper*

Tell the children about how a star can be found in the middle of an apple. Then cut apples apart horizontally, vertically and in slices. Dip in paint and make apple prints. Make up a story about how the star got in the center of the apple.

Snack Time

You'll need:

- *apples*
- *spoons*
- *large bowl*
- *small bowls*
- *cinnamon*
- *potato masher*
- *plastic knives*
- *cutting board*
- *large electric skillet*

Peel the apples and cut into slices. Let the children use the plastic knives to dice several slices. Put all the diced apples in the skillet. Steam them with a small amount of cinnamon and water. When the apples are soft, transfer them to a large bowl and let each student have a turn mashing. Cool and spoon into small bowls for each child to enjoy.

Be sure to take time to compare the texture and taste of cooked apples to fresh apples.

Ready to Rest

Here's a rhyme to learn and say together right before quiet time.

"An apple a day,
Plus some rest and some play,
Helps me grow more each day,
In my own special way."

APPLE DAY PLAY

Music & Movement

Yummy Apples (Sing to tune of *Row, Row, Row Your Boat*)

Red, green, yellow red,
The apples taste so sweet.
I love to eat one every day.
It really is a treat!

Tree Fell Down from ***Easy Does It*** by Hap Palmer (see Resources, page 7), provides the background for children to pretend they are moving under and around an apple tree.

Science

Cut an apple in half. Take out the seeds. Talk about what the seeds are for. Count how many there are. Repeat the process with another apple and compare the results. Plant the seeds in a dish of soil and watch them closely for growth over the next few weeks.

Skill Builder: Letter Recognition

Cut a large red, green or yellow construction paper apple for each student. Have them glue the paper apple to another piece of construction paper then color a brown stem and green leaf.

Use a black crayon to write the letter "A" in the center of the apple. Practice saying the letter and explain that the word apple starts with the sound of the letter "A".

Motor Development

You'll need:
- *parachute or large sheet*
- *red, green and yellow foam balls*

Seat the children in a circle around the parachute. Have them hold onto the edges with their fingers on top and thumbs "hiding" underneath. Practice moving the parachute up and down. Use position words to help direct them. "Move the parachute *over* your head."

Now tell the children you are going to make something with apples such as apple pie or applesauce. Invite them to volunteer a "recipe". Place the foam "apples" on the parachute. Pretend to add the other ingredients. Mix the ingredients by moving the parachute. Challenge the children to keep all the apples on the parachute.

As a variation, try to get rid of the "rotten apples". Choose one of the colors to get off the parachute while leaving the others on.

Closing

Seat the children in a group. Ask three or four to hold an apple. Play a favorite song. As the music plays, the children pass the apples around the group. When the music stops, the children holding the apples line up to go home. Continue play until everyone is in line.

BALLOON DAY PLAY

The Sky Is The Limit On Balloon Day!

GETTING READY:

5 Days before Balloon Day, send out the parent information notice provided. One day prior to the event, send home the reminder notice.

You will need these materials for Balloon Day Play *Activities:*

Opening :
- Extra balloons

Art Corner:
- Tempera paint
- Brushes
- Scissors
- Construction paper squares
- Pictures of hot-air balloons
- Painting paper

Snack Time:
- Small balloon for each child
- Permanent marker
- String
- Snack food in package

Motor Development
- Balloons
- Net or line
- Lightweight paddles

Literature Corner and Music:
- See suggested titles in activities

Science:
- String
- Drinking straws
- Masking tape
- Balloons

BALLOON DAY PLAY

We are planning a special theme day. Please read the information below and gather all the requested items to send with your child on the date indicated below.

Date:______________________

Please send: One deflated balloon, any size and color

Other needs:

A reminder will be sent home on the day prior to the special event.

If you would be willing to help, please sign and return this form with your child.________________

BALLOON DAY PLAY

Reminder

Tomorrow is our special Balloon Day. **Please remember to send** a balloon, any size and color, with your child and any other materials requested on our original notice. (Do not blow up the balloon.) If you have any questions, please feel free to call me at ____________________.

And remember to ask your child to share the learning fun they had on Balloon Day!

Sincerely,

BALLOON DAY PLAY

THE DAY'S ACTIVITIES

Opening

Ask each child to bring you the balloon they brought to school. Name the color. Ask them to show with their arms, the size and shape they think their balloon will be when it is blown up.

Literature Corner

Share some adventure books about balloons:

The Great Town and Country Bicycle Balloon Chase **by Barbara Douglass,** Lothrop, Lee & Shepard Books, 1984
Gina and Grandpa are on a balloon chase but end up with a parrot.

Bear's Adventure **by Brian Wildsmith;** Pantheon Books, 1981
A bear has an adventure that begins and ends in a hot air balloon.

Skill Builder: Size & Shape Comparison

Blow up all of the balloons the children brought to school. Compare the size, shape and colors of the balloons.

Skill Builder: Counting

After completing the comparison activity above, count how many balloons are in each shape, size or color category.

You'll need:

- *tempera paint*
- *brushes*
- *pictures of hot air balloons*
- *large sheets of painting paper*
- *scissors*
- *construction paper squares*

Before beginning the art project, share pictures of hot air balloons with the children. Talk about the bright colors and designs they see in the balloons. Have them paint a large sheet of paper with any colors and designs they choose. When dry, cut out a large balloon shape. Create a wall display by mounting the painted balloon and positioning a square of construction paper underneath for the balloon basket.

Snack Time

You'll Need:

- *string or tape*
- *balloon for each child*
- *snack food in package*
- *permanent marker*

Write a child's name in bold lettering on each balloon. Tie or tape the balloon to a snack food. Have each child find the balloon with his or her name on it. Help those who need name recognition assistance. Enjoy the snack together.

Ready to Rest

As the children are lying down to rest and relax, ask them to close their eyes and imagine that they are gently floating through the sky on a balloon. Ask them to visualize the things they see below and around them. Have them imagine a soft, cool breeze on their face.

BALLOON DAY PLAY

Music

Our Balloons (Sing to tune of *Pop Goes the Weasel.*)

Our balloons are red and green,
Blue and yellow too.
Please be careful with them all,
Or they might pop at you!

Colorful Balloons (Sing to tune of *Freres Jacques.*)

We have red balloons,
Yellow, green and blue.
How about you?
How about you?

We can hit them up and down,
We can hit them all around.
You try it too!
You try it too!

Science

You'll need:

- *18-inch (45 cm) length of string*
- *deflated balloon*
- *drinking straw*
- *masking tape*

Thread the string through the length of the straw. Tape a deflated balloon to the side of the straw so it is secure but can still be inflated. Blow up the balloon and pinch the opening closed to keep the air inside. Have children hold each end of the string. Slide the straw to one end. Let the balloon go and see how far the straw travels on the string. Mark the spot and try again. Does the balloon always travel to the same spot? What makes it move?

Repeat the activity with two balloons and string at the same time.

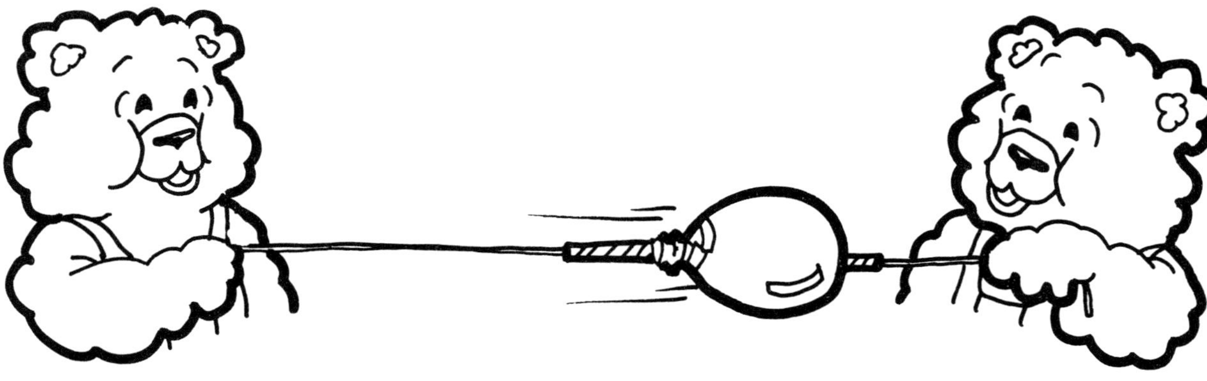

Motor Development

You'll need:

- *balloon for each child*
- *lightweight racket or Whammer Bammer (from* ***Make It Today for Pre-K Play****. See Resources, page 6.) Use the palm of the hands if neither type of racket is available.*

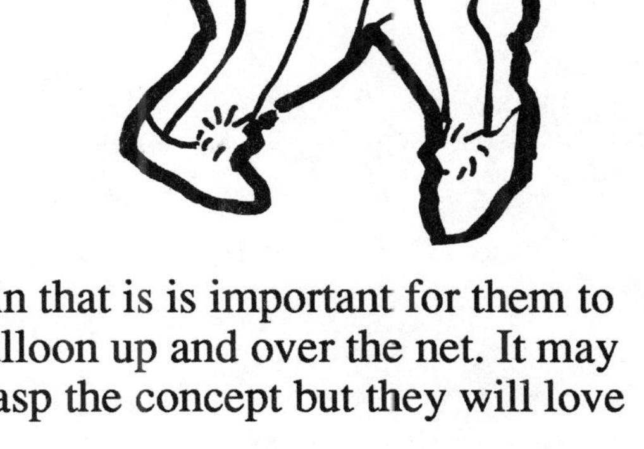

Develop eye-hand coordination by hitting the balloon gently with the Whammer Bammer, a lightweight racket, or the palm of the hand. Be sure you have plenty of space for the children to move around safely. Demonstrate how to hit the balloon with an upward motion.

Now play a game together. String a net across the play area. If a net is not available, tie a string between two chairs. Tie scarves or streamers from the string to make it look more like a net. Space the children on each side of the net in the playing area. Seat them cross-legged and explain that is is important for them to stay in their own space. Hit the balloon up and over the net. It may take a while for the children to grasp the concept but they will love playing this over and over.

Closing

Give each child a balloon to hold. (If the ones with their names on them are still intact, you may give them those.) Say a color. If a child is holding that color balloon, they may float like a balloon to get ready to go home.

Clown Around And Learn, Too!

GETTING READY:

5 Days before Circus Day, send out the parent information notice provided. One day prior to the event, send home the reminder notice.

You will need these materials for Circus Day Play *Activities:*

Opening :
- "Clown" dress-up clothes

Art Corner:
- Tongue depressors
- Crayons
- Construction paper
- White glue, yarn, glitter, trims
- Scissors, construction paper
- Animal templates or pictures

Snack Time:
- Rice cakes • Peanut Butter
- Coconut, raisins, small candies
- Plastic knives

Motor Development
- Bean bags
- Music: See activity

Literature Corner and Music:
- See suggested titles in activities

Skill Builders:
- Non-toxic makeup
- Watercolors, brushes
- Mirrors
- Circus-related animal pictures
- Dress-up clothing

CIRCUS DAY PLAY

We are planning a special theme day. Please read the information below and gather all the requested items to send with your child on the date indicated below.

Date:____________________

Please send: An article of clothing that might be worn by a clown .

Other needs:

A reminder will be sent home on the day prior to the special event.

If you would be willing to help, please sign and return this form with your child.______________

CIRCUS DAY PLAY

Reminder

Tomorrow is our special Circus Day. **Please remember to send** an article of clothing that might be worn by a clown with your child and any other materials requested on our original notice. If you have any questions, please feel free to call me at

____________________.

And remember to ask your child to share the learning fun they had on Popcorn Day!

Sincerely,

THE DAY'S ACTIVITIES

Opening

Ask each child to share the article of clothing they brought that a clown might wear. Have them put on the item. Talk about each one. Is it a floppy hat? A wild tie? Big, big shoes?

Share some circus memories. How many of them have been to a circus? Describe what they might see there.

Literature Corner

Have a three-ring circus story time. Suggested books:

C is For Circus **by Bernice Chardiet**; Walker and Company, 1971
Each letter of the alphabet is represented with a circus item.

Circus **by Brian Wildsmith**, Franklin Watts Inc, 1970
With very few words, circus-fun is brought to town.

Curious George Goes to the Circus **by Margaret & H.A. Rey**, Houghton Mifflin, 1984
George, the monkey, steals the show with his mischievous acts.

Skill Builder: Creative Movement

Encourage each child to share something they might see at the circus. It might be a roaring lion, a lumbering elephant or a high-flying trapeze artist.

Ask them—or let them choose a willing volunteer—to act out what was shared. The rest of the children try to follow the movement.

Art Corner

You'll need:

- *tongue depressors or craft sticks*
- *construction paper*
- *animal templates or pictures*
- *white glue, scissors, crayons*
- *glitter, yarn, and other trims*

Create animal stick puppets using the art materials supplied. Have an impromptu puppet show with the finished projects.

Snack Time

You'll Need:

- *rice cakes*
- *plastic knives*
- *peanut butter*
- *raisins, chocolate chips, M&Ms, coconut, etc.*

Give each child a rice cake on which to spread peanut butter. Set out the food items and invite them to create a clown face in the peanut butter on the rice cake.

Let everyone share their clown creation before eating!

Ready to Rest

Clowning around can be exhausting work! When your clowns are ready for a rest, recite this rhyme:

"Lions, tigers, bears and clowns.
All of them moving up and down.
They roar and growl and don't want to stop,
Until they find a place to rest and FLOP!"

CIRCUS DAY PLAY

Music

Kids' Circus by Georgiana Liccione Stewart (see Resources, page 7) is loaded with music for this special day. Each song has something different to do with the circus. Use the music as background for your circus parade, animal pantomimes or just sharing stories about the circus and memories under the "Big Top".

Skill Builder: Auditory Memory

Gather together in a group for some listening skill development. Recite a series of circus actions to perform. "Swing your arms like a monkey and prance like a horse." "Roar like a lion and swing your trunk like an elephant."

Start with two actions then add more to suit student ability.

Skill Builder: Creative Dramatics

You'll need:

- *non-toxic makeup*
- *mirrors*
- *watercolors, brushes*
- *clown dress-up clothing*

It's "create a clown" time. Let each child choose a partner or make up their own face to look like a clown.

Wear your clown clothing then parade through other classrooms (or the neighborhood) to show off your classroom full of clowns.

Motor Development

You'll need:
- *bean bag for each child*
- *music, as specified below (See Resources, page 7)*

Since clowns are so well-known for their juggling, its' time to try your hand at the trick. Play some music for inspiration!

Make Friends With a Bean Bag from ***Bean Bag Activities and Coordination Skills*** by Georgiana Liccione Stewart

Bean Bag Juggle from ***Me and My Bean Bag*** by the Learning Station

Skill Builder: Visual Memory

Conduct a three-ring memory circus. Draw three circles (rings) on a chalkboard. Have tape and circus-related animal pictures available. Tape a picture inside each ring. Let the children study the pictures for a moment.

Remove the pictures and ask for a volunteer to replace the pictures in the same rings.

After playing a couple times, involve students in the picture placement and removal.

Closing

Put all the clown clothing the children brought in the middle of a seated group. Ask each child to move like a circus animal, retrieve their clothing and get ready to go home when you call their name.

POPCORN DAY PLAY

GetLearning Popping With Popcorn!

GETTING READY:

5 Days before Popcorn Day, send out the parent information notice provided. One day prior to the event, send home the reminder notice.

You will need these materials for Popcorn Day Play *Activities:*

Opening :
- Popcorn and popper

Art Corner:
- Brown lunch bags
- Powdered tempera paint
- Construction paper
- White glue
- Popped corn

Snack Time:
- Cooking Oil
- Napkins
- Popper
- Popcorn kernels

Motor Development
- 8-10 ping-pong balls
- Parachute or large sheet
- Music: See suggestions

Literature Corner:
- Book: See suggested titles.

Skill Builders:
- Small jars

Science
- Magnifying glass

POPCORN DAY PLAY

We are planning a special theme day. Please read the information below and gather all the requested items to send with your child on the date indicated below.

Date:_____________________

Please send: A half bag of popcorn
Other needs:

A reminder will be sent home on the day prior to the special event.

If you would be willing to help please sign and return this form with your child._______________

POPCORN DAY PLAY

Reminder

Tomorrow is our special Popcorn Day. **Please remember to send** a half bag of popcorn with your child and any other materials requested on our original notice. If you have any questions, please feel free to call me at ____________________.

And remember to ask your child to share the learning fun they had on Popcorn Day!

Sincerely,

THE DAY'S ACTIVITIES

Opening

Pop popcorn in the room before the children arrive so the room smells good when they enter it. (Save the popped corn for the day's activities.) Encourage creative thinking during morning group. Ask the children what they smelled when they entered the room. What does the smell of popcorn make them think of? How would it feel to be a kernel of corn being popped?

Music

Popcorn's Popping (Sing to tune of *Twinkle, Twinkle Little Star*)

Popcorn, popcorn pop up high,
Popcorn, popcorn fall from the sky.
Popcorn, popcorn your kernels shine bright,
Popcorn, popcorn you're turning white.
Popcorn, popcorn pop up high,
Popcorn, popcorn fall from the sky.

Skill Builder: Shapes & Directionality

Tell the children they are going on a popcorn maze walk. Use popcorn to create a path to follow. Make arrows from the popcorn to follow and drop popcorn to mark the way. Make basic shapes out of the popcorn as part of the path. Plan a skill to do at each shape such as hop two times when you see a square, stand beside all circles, balance on one foot inside all triangles. Mark the end of the path with a sticker.

Art Corner

You'll need:

- *small brown paper lunch bags*
- *powdered tempera paint*
- *popped corn*
- *construction paper*
- *white glue*

Place three tablespoons of powdered tempera in a paper bag. Add popcorn to fill half the bag. Close the bag and shake. Remove the popcorn. Glue the colored popcorn to construction paper to create a picture or design.

Snack Time

You'll Need:

- *popcorn popper*
- *oil*
- *napkins*
- *popcorn kernels*
- *large sheet or towel*

Place the sheet in a large open area. Put the popper in the middle. Seat children around the towel, safely spaced from the popper. Follow directions for popping corn but do not put the lid on. Let the kernels pop freely over the towel. Be sure the children know to remain seated while the corn is popping.

You can make popcorn balls, too, by melting a bag of marshmallows with a stick of butter. Add popcorn. Give each child a small amount to shape into a ball. Coat hands lightly with oil.

Ready to Rest

As the children are thinking about all the different things they were able to do with a kernel of popcorn, say:

"Popcorn, popcorn, you've smelled so good.
I've tasted you, made something and played with you too".
I know we're both tired so let's take a rest,
And then when we get up we'll both be at our best!"

POPCORN DAY PLAY

Literature Corner

Munch on some popcorn during story time. Suggested books:

The Popcorn Book **by Tomi De Paola;** Holiday, 1978
Fun recipes and stories about the origin of popcorn.

Popcorn **by Frank Asch,;**Parents, 1979
Little bear hosts a Halloween Party and manages to fill the entire house with popcorn.

Science

You'll need:
- *Magnifying glasses*

Place an unpopped kernel of corn next to a popped one. Compare the difference. What do the children think happened to the kernel of corn to make it change? Provide magnifying glasses to examine the popped and unpopped kernels.

Skill Builder: Counting, Estimating

You'll need:
- *small baby food jar*
- *popcorn kernels to fill jar*
- *popcorn popper*
- *oil*

Fill the jar with popcorn kernels. Let children guess how many they think are in the jar. Help them write their guess on a piece of chart paper. Count the kernels in the jar together. Compare the guesses to the actual number.

Put popped corn back into the jar. Count how many times you can fill the jar with the popped corn.

Motor Development

You'll need:

- *parachute or large sheet*
- *8-10 ping-pong balls*

Spread a parachute on the floor. Seat children around the edge. Ask them to recall what was needed to make popcorn and pretend to put them on the parachute. The ping ball "kernels" should be last.

While seated, grasp the edge of the parachute with fingers on top and thumbs underneath. Slowly move the parachute up and down. Then move faster and faster to get the corn popping. Soon you will have popcorn popping everywhere. You might like to play *Popcorn* from ***We All Live Together*** (see resources, page 7) while making parachute popcorn.

Remind children to stay seated. Choose a few to bring the "popped corn" back to the parachute, being very careful to watch where they are stepping. Now you are ready to pop some more popcorn.

Closing

Listen to *The Freeze* from ***We All Live Together.*** (See resources, page 7.) While the music plays, children pretend they are a kernel of popping corn. When the music stops, curl up in a ball and become an unpopped kernel. Invite children, one at a time, to be a popping kernel as they gather their things and get ready to go home.

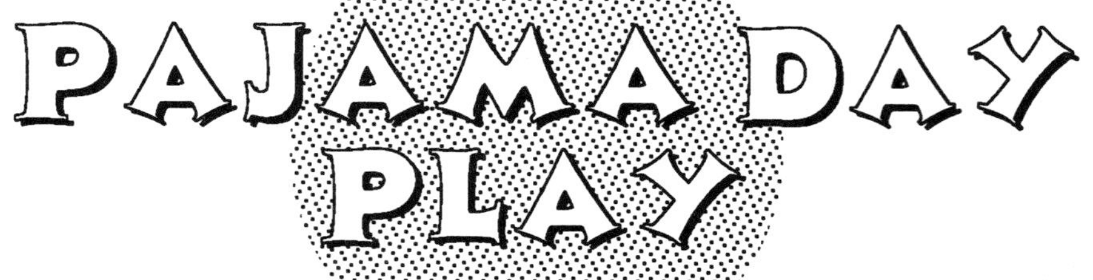

PAJAMA DAY PLAY

Sweet Dreams For Little Learners!

GETTING READY:

5 Days before Pajama Day, send out the parent information notice provided. One day prior to the event, send home the reminder notice.

You will need these materials for Pajama Day Play *Activities:*

Opening
- Extra pajama tops

Art Corner:
- Cardboard gift boxes
- Tissue paper scraps
- White glue
- Tempera paint, assorted colors

Snack Time:
- Cereal
- Plastic spoons
- Milk
- Bowls

Motor Development
- Pillows
- Pillow case for each pillow

Science:
- Book about animals sleeping (See literature suggestions)

Literature Corner and Music:
- See suggested titles in activities

Skill Builders:
- Bedtime props: toothbrush, toothpaste, soap, blanket, etc.
- Sheet

PAJAMA DAY PLAY

We are planning a special theme day. Please read the information below and gather all the requested items to send with your child on the date indicated below.

Date:____________________

Please send: Child to school in pajamas; favorite bedtime book

Other needs:

A reminder will be sent home on the day prior to the special event.

If you would be willing to help, please sign and return this form with your child.______________

PAJAMA DAY PLAY

Reminder

Tomorrow is our special Pajama Day. **Please remember to send** your child in pajamas, a favorite bedtime book and any other materials requested on our original notice. If you have any questions, please feel free to call me at ___________________.

And remember to ask your child to share the learning fun they had on Popcorn Day!

Sincerely,

PAJAMA DAY PLAY

THE DAY'S ACTIVITIES

During morning group let each child have a turn to model the pajamas they wore and tell what is their favorite thing about this particular pair of pajamas. Choose two books to read from the bedtime favorites that children brought. Ask the child who brought the book to help you turn the pages and share the book with classmates.

Literature Corner

Share some "nighttime" books:

Ira Sleeps Over **by Bernard Waber,** Houghton Mifflin, 1972
Ira is afraid his friend will laugh at his teddy bear.

Goodnight Moon **by Margaret Wise Brown**, Harper LB, 1979
Get ready to sleep as you say goodnight to everything in the room.

The Goodnight Circle **by Carolyn Lesser**, Harcourt Brace Jovanovich, 1984
Describes different animals' sleeping habits.

Skill Builder: Sequencing

Have on hand some of the things children might use when getting ready for bed. Some suggestions are a toothbrush, toothpaste, washcloth, soap, book, glass of water and blanket.

Ask children to recall and share their bedtime routines. Use the props to act them out.

You'll need:

- *cardboard gift box*
- *tempera paint, assorted colors*
- *paint brushes*
- *tissue paper scraps*
- *white glue*

Be sure each child selects a box top or bottom large enough for a favorite stuffed animal to "lie" in. Decorate the box with tissue paper scraps.

Turn the box into a bed to take home to tuck a favorite stuffed animal into at bedtime.

Snack Time

You'll Need:

- *cereal assortment*
- *milk*
- *plastic spoons*
- *bowls*

Pretend you're just starting out your morning and have breakfast cereal for snack. Develop your auditory senses by listening to the sounds the cereal makes when milk is poured over. How would students describe the sounds? While eating, tell about your favorite kind of cereal.

Ready to Rest

Play some relaxing music while children snuggle down for a rest. Select a few more student-favorite bedtime books to read aloud.

You may want to sing a lullaby together, too.

PAJAMA DAY PLAY

Music

Gentle, relaxing music is appropriate for the day's activities. See Resources, page 7, for details about these musical suggestions.

Sweet Dreams: Restful Music for Quite Times

Quiet Moments With Greg and Steve, Youngheart Records

Spaghetti Test from ***Learning Through Movement and Song*** by Sheri Senter.

Science

Share a book about animal sleeping habits (See literature titles). Find out what animals sleep during the day and are awake at night. What animals are heard first thing in the morning? Where do animals sleep and in what position do they sleep? Choose some animals to pantomime while they are asleep.

Skill Builder: Visual Memory

Choose a student to stand before the class. Ask those still seated to study the pajamas (or sleepwear) worn by the student in front.

After a moment, cover the child with a blanket. Ask seated students to describe the pajamas the child was wearing.

What colors do they remember? Were there any shapes or pictures on them? Were there buttons, zippers, trims? Did they notice any holes or worn spots? What length were the sleeves?

Motor Development

You'll need:

- *several pillows*
- *pillow case for each pillow*

Practice putting a pillow into a pillow case. Start by working in pairs then master the movement individually. When all children can successfully put a pillow in a pillow case, play a relay game.

Divide into teams. Place a pillow and a pillow case a distance from the starting line. Each team participant must "sleepwalk" to the pillow, put it completely in its case and take it out of the case again before returning to the starting position.

Skill Builder: Recall

Do this activity towards the end of the day after you have read many of the books brought by the children.

Spend some time recalling and retelling the stories they remember that have been read so far.

Choose a couple more of the books to read now.

Closing

Gather together again for another opportunity to share a few more of the books brought by children. After reading, call on several children by name and ask them to "sleepwalk" to get their things ready to go home.

Your Class Will Bubble With Excitement!

GETTING READY:

5 Days before Bubble Day, send out the parent information notice provided. One day prior to the event, send home the reminder notice.

You will need these materials for Bubble Day Play *Activities:*

Opening :
- Bubble solution
  See recipe. Make the night before or two hours prior.

Art Corner:
- White construction paper
- Drinking straws
- Egg Beater, bowl
- Liquid soap • Food coloring

Snack Time:
- Fruit juice • Sparkling water
- Clear plastic cups

Motor Development
- Variety of store-bought & homemade bubble wands
  See suggestions in activities

Literature Corner:
- Book: See suggested titles

Skill Builders:
- Large paper "bubbles"
- Liquid soap • Water

Science
- Large, wide-mouth glass jar
- Plastic tubing • Straws
- Collection of small items

BUBBLE DAY PLAY

We are planning a special theme day. Please read the information below and gather all the requested items to send with your child on the date indicated below.

Date:_______________________

Please send: A bottle of bubble solution and wand
Other needs:

A reminder will be sent home on the day prior to the special event.

If you would be willing to help, please sign and return this form with your child.________________

BUBBLE DAY PLAY

Reminder

Tomorrow is our special Bubble Day. **Please remember to send** a jar of bubble solution and wand with your child and any other materials requested on our original notice. If you have any questions, please feel free to call me at ____________________.

And remember to ask your child to share the learning fun they had on Bubble Day!

Sincerely,

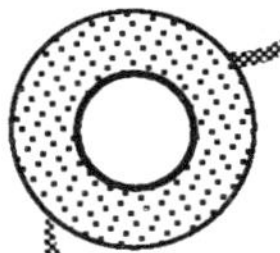

BUBBLE DAY PLAY

THE DAY'S ACTIVITIES

Opening

Blow bubbles in the air and call a child's name to come and pop them. Ask them what it felt like to pop a bubble.

Literature Corner

Float like a bubble and find a soft place to land for story time. Suggested books:

King Bidgood's in the Bathtub **by Audrey Wood,** Harcourt Brace, 1985
The king is taking a bubble bath and no one can get him out.

The Magic Bubble Trip **by Ingrid & Dieter Schubert,** Kane Miller, 1985
A tale of a trip in a magical bubble.

Skill Builder: Directionality, Spatial Awareness

Making a large batch of bubble soap.

You'll need:

- *6 cups water*
- *2 cups Dawn liquid soap (Other brands can be used but are not as effective.)*

Mix the two ingredients. Allow them to set for a minimum of two hours. If possible, make the mixture the night before.

Blow bubbles outside in an open area. Have children identify bubbles as being small, medium or large in size. Ask them if the bubble landed in front of or behind their body.

Challenge children to catch a bubble in the palm of their hand without popping it. Try catching one in front, alongside or behind the body.

Art Corner

You'll need:

- *1/4 cup Dawn liquid dish soap (this brand is most successful.)*
- *food coloring*
- *white construction paper*
- *drinking straws*
- *egg beater, bowl*

Place two cups water, liquid soap and a few drops of food coloring in a bowl. (Powdered tempera paint may be substituted for food coloring.) Children may blow into a straw or use an egg beater to make bubbles in the mixture. (If using straws, be sure children understand they are to blow, not suck.)

When enough bubbles have been blown to reach the rim of the bowl, place a piece of white paper across the top of the bowl to make a bubble print. Stir the liquid mixture after each print. For variety, provide bowls with different color mixtures. Children may create a picture using the color combination of their choice.

Snack Time

You'll Need:

- *two different kinds of fruit juice*
- *sparkling water*
- *clear plastic cups*

Add sparkling water to your favorite fruit juice. Observe and describe the bubbles in the juice? Does the taste change?

Ready to Rest

While the children are settling for a rest, say:

"A bubble sails and floats through the air
Then slowly disappears.
Do not be sad, for you can make a new friend,
Right after you rest and fill yourself with new cheer!"

BUBBLE DAY PLAY

Science

You'll need:
- *large, wide-mouth glass jar*
- *3-4 feet, 1/4-inch, plastic tubing (available in hardware stores)*
- *drinking straw to fit inside tubing*
- *small items to fit into jar (coins, corks, plastic toys, etc.)*

Make a bubble jar by filling the jar half way with water. Add the small items. Place one end of the tubing into the water. Insert a straw into the other end of the tubing. Blow into the straw. Bubbles should appear in the water. What do the bubbles do to the items in the jar?

Music

Play a slow song from Hap Palmer's recording ***Movin'*** (See Resources page 7.) Invite the children to float and glide around the room (or play area) like a bubble in the air.

Skill Builder: Counting

Have each child take a turn at blowing bubbles. The rest of the class tries to count how many bubbles were blown from one dip of the wand into the solution.

The child who blew the bubbles can write their name on a paper bubble along with the number of bubbles blown. Hang the bubbles around the classroom. Use the bubbles later to reinforce number recognition. "Stand under the bubble that has the number six on it."

Motor Development

You'll need various sized bubble blowing wands, including:

- *plastic six -pack holder*
- *large rubber bands*
- *three drinking straws taped together*

Designate a bubble blowing area. Explore the many different implements and techniques that can be used to blow bubbles. Challenge children to run among the bubbles and not be caught! Once a bubble bursts on the body, the child sits down and stays seated until everyone has been "caught" by a bubble.

Closing

Repeat the opening activity with a variation. When a child's name is called, name a body part. The child must try to pop a bubble using that body part. Older children can receive a more challenging assignment such as popping a bubble between their hand and knee or by touching it with their nose. After the child's turn they should float like a bubble and get ready to go home.

Make Scarves A Learning Accessory !

GETTING READY:

5 Days before Scarf Day, send out the parent information notice provided. One day prior to the event, send home the reminder notice.

You will need these materials for Scarf Day Play *Activities:*

Opening :
- Extra scarves

Art Corner:
- Fabric scraps
- Construction paper
- White glue
- Fabric Scissors
- Watercolors and brushes

Snack Time:
- Fruit rollups • Boxed juice

Skill Builders
- Tray
- 4-7 small items
- Tape measure
- Scarf

Literature Corner and Music:
- See suggested titles in activities

SCARF DAY PLAY

We are planning a special theme day. Please read the information below and gather all the requested items to send with your child on the date indicated below.

Date:______________________

Please send: A scarf labeled with your child's name.

Other needs:

A reminder will be sent home on the day prior to the special event.

If you would be willing to help, please sign and return this form with your child.________________

SCARF DAY PLAY

Reminder

Tomorrow is our special Scarf Day. **Please remember to send** a scarf labeled with your child's name and any other materials requested on our original notice. If you have any questions, please feel free to call me at ____________________.

And remember to ask your child to share the learning fun they had on Scarf Day!

Sincerely,

THE DAY'S ACTIVITIES

Opening

Give each child an opportunity to share the scarf they brought to school. Talk about the colors in each one. Hold them open and compare the shapes. Are they long? Short? Square? Rectangle?

Literature Corner

Read the story then invite children, one at a time, to walk around the reading circle and drop their scarf in front of a person they would like to have as a new friend.

The Wedding of Brown Bear and White Bear **by Martin Beck,** Little Brown, 1989
White Bear sends her scarf in answer to a marriage proposal.

Snack Time

You'll Need:
- *fruit rollups*
- *boxed drinks*

Gather the children's scarves. Put the snack in the center of each open scarf. Pull the corners to the center and tie them in the middle. Ask each child to find their scarf bundle with its snack surprise.

Skill Builder: Directionality

Ask the children to move their scarves to the right, left, up and down. They can also be asked to move the scarf above or over their head, below their waist or behind their back.

Art Corner

You'll need:

- *fabric scissors*
- *fabric scraps*
- *white glue*
- *construction paper*
- *watercolors and brushes*

In preparation, cut fabric scraps into small scarf shapes—triangles, squares and rectangles.

Have children paint a watercolor picture of an animal or person. Let them select a fabric scarf shape to glue to the picture. If there is enough fabric, cut a matching scarf for the painter!.

Skill Builder: Creative Thinking

Give the picture painted during art a chance to dry. Ask the artist to dictate a sentence or short story about their painting. Encourage them to include themselves in the story if they have a matching fabric scarf. Write their response on the painting. Ask volunteers to share their story.

To further develop creative thinking, oral language and sequencing, select a picture to share with the class. Build a story about the picture together. You may need to begin with an opening sentence to get them started.

Ready to Rest

As the children move their scarves, say this rhyme, then rest awhile.

"My scarf can move high and some times very low.
It knows how to fly both fast and slow.
It is ready to rest and I know so am I.
So I'll put my head on my scarf and close my sleepy eyes."

SCARF DAY PLAY

Skill Builder: Measurement

You'll need:
- *tape measure*

Have the children bring their scarf for a cooperative activity. Ask them how long they think you could measure if all the scarves were tied together. After some discussion, tie the scarves together, end to end. Practice small motor skills, too, while children learn to tie a knot. When all the scarves are tied together, ask the children for help in straightening it out. Have a child walk the length. Count the steps as they walk. Use a measuring tape to measure the length.

Untie all the scarves. Have children take their own scarf and find something in the room that measures the same length.

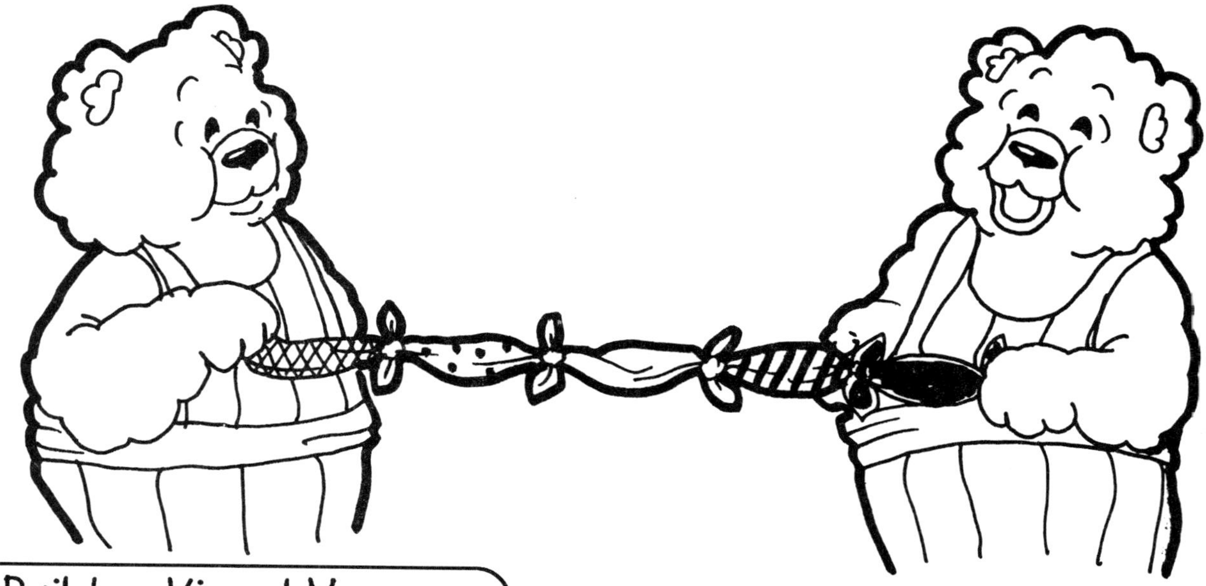

Skill Builder: Visual Memory

You'll need:
- *tray with several small items on it*
- *scarf*

Ask the children sit in a group. Show them a tray with several items on it. Talk about the items. Cover the tray with a scarf. Reach your hand under the scarf and remove an item without them seeing what it is. Take off the scarf and show the children the tray once again. Ask them to name the missing item. Continue play while interests lasts. Increase the number of items on the tray and the number removed.

Get Students In Good Learning Shape !

GETTING READY:

5 Days before Shape Day, send out the parent information notice provided. One day prior to the event, send home the reminder notice.

You will need these materials for Shape Day Play *Activities:*

Opening :
- Fabric with shape prints

Skill Builders:
- Paper shapes
- Sponge shapes
- Fingerpaint
- Art paper

Art Corner:
- Scissors for each child
- White glue
- Crayons or markers
- Construction paper
- Shapes traced on construction paper

Game Time:
- Plastic or wire hoops

Snack Time:
- Cheese slices
- Stick pretzels
- Bananas
- Plastic knives
- Square-shaped crackers

Motor Development
- Foam rubber or sponge shapes

Literature Corner and Music:
- See suggested titles in activities

SHAPE DAY PLAY

We are planning a special theme day. Please read the information below and gather all the requested items to send with your child on the date indicated below.

Date:____________________

Please send: Your child dressed in clothing that has shapes in the fabric—polka dots, plaids, etc.

Other needs:

A reminder will be sent home on the day prior to the special event.

If you would be willing to help, please sign and return this form with your child.______________

SHAPE DAY PLAY

Reminder

Tomorrow is our special Shape Day. **Please remember to** have your child dressed in clothing that has shapes in the fabric—polka dots, plaids, logos and insignias, for example, plus any other materials requested on our original notice. If you have questions, please call me at

_____________.

And remember to ask your child to share the learning fun they had on Shape Day!

Sincerely,

THE DAY'S ACTIVITIES

Opening

Ask each child to come to school wearing clothing with shapes in the fabric. Stand up, one by one, and let their classmates name the shapes they see.

Have them look closely for polka dot circles, squares and rectangles found in plaids and shapes that are part of logos and insignias.

Literature Corner

Round and Round and Round **by Tana Hobin,** Greenwillow Books, 1983
A color photographic book featuring things that are round.

Shapes, Shapes, Shapes **by Tana Hobin**, Greenwillow Books, 1986
A color photographic book featuring many shapes.

Art Corner

You'll need:

- *scissors for each child*
- *construction paper*
- *shapes traced on construction paper*
- *white glue*
- *crayons or markers*

Make a shape picture. Cut out the traced, construction paper shapes and glue them to another colorful sheet of construction paper. Use crayons or markers to add details.

Skill Builder: Visual Recognition

Name a shape then ask a child to find something that shape in the room. If they can, bring the item back to the group. If the item is too large they should stand by it until everyone has had a turn.

Snack Time

You'll Need:

- *cheese slices*
- *plastic knife for each child*
- *square shaped crackers such as saltines*
- *bananas*
- *stick pretzels*

Have children make a basic-shape snack! Slice the banana into circles. Use the knife to cut a rectangular piece of cheese. Add a square cracker. Use three pretzels to form a triangle. Can they name the shapes they made? Call out a shape and have them eat that one!

More Movement: Shape Walk

Give each child a shape and a marker. Vary the shapes so that there are as many different ones as possible. Go for a walk around the school area. Every time a child sees something that is the shape they are holding they should make a mark on their shape.

When you return to the room count the marks together and find out which shape can be found the most around your school.

Game Time

You'll need:

- *Hoop Loop for each child*
  *(See **Make It Today for Pre-K Play**, Resources, page 6)*
  If this equipment is not available, use another circular shape such as a bent wire frame or Hula Hoop.

Place the hoops around the room. Play the song *Jump and Land* from ***Learning With Circles and Sticks*** by Hap Palmer. (See Resources, page 7.) Follow the words to the song to play the game.

If the music is not available, create your own game using the circular hoops. Children may jump from one to another, complete a specified motion in each hoop or sing a song as they play follow the leader from one hoop to another. Instrumental background music may be selected.

Skill Builder: Auditory Memory

You'll need:

- *variety of shapes cut from foam rubber, styrofoam, or sponges—each child will need a set*

Ask the children to line up or stack shapes in a certain order or pattern such as circle, square, triangle, circle, rectangle.

Use the shapes with directional commands giving more than one direction at a time. For example, "Place a circle in front of the triangle and a square next to the triangle."

Skill Builder: Shapes, Patterns

You'll Need:
- *fingerpaints*
- *art paper*
- *variety of construction paper shapes*

Discuss and share shape patterns with the children. Use the paper shapes as visual props to create several patterns for them to see. Ask the children to work duplicate the shape pattern by fingerpainting it on art paper.

You may prefer to eliminate the fingerpainting step and simply provide children with cut paper shapes with which to duplicate the pattern.

Motor Development

You'll need:
- *shapes made from foam rubber or other sturdy material*

Shapes in Action by Georgiana Liccione Stewart, (See Resources, page 7), provides music that involves children in shape activities reinforcing triangle, square and circle recognition. The songs are fairly easy for children to follow along using their foam rubber shapes. Younger children may find greater success using the instrumental side of the album with teacher-created instructions set to children's learning pace.

Closing

Give each child a paper shape. Call the name of a shape. Everyone holding that paper shape puts it in a bucket you have ready for them and gets ready to go home.

Start Learning Off With A Roar !

GETTING READY:

5 Days before Animal Day, send out the parent information notice provided. One day prior to the event, send home the reminder notice.

You will need these materials for Animal Day Play *Activities:*

Opening :
- Extra stuffed animals for those who forgot theirs

Art Corner:
- Cardboard box for each child, large enough to hold their stuffed animal
- Tempera paint in a variety of colors
- Paint brushes
- Collage materials
- Crepe paper streamers
- Yarn • White glue

Snack Time:
- Animal crackers

Motor Development
- Parachute or large sheet
- Music: See activity

Literature Corner and Music:
- See suggested titles in activities

ANIMAL DAY PLAY

We are planning a special theme day. Please read the information below and gather all the requested items to send with your child on the date indicated below.

Date:_____________________

Please send: A stuffed animal

Other needs:

A reminder will be sent home on the day prior to the special event.

If you would be willing to help, please sign and return this form with your child._______________

ANIMAL DAY PLAY

Reminder

Tomorrow is our special Animal Day. **Please remember to send** a stuffed animal with your child and any other materials requested on our original notice. If you have any questions, please feel free to call me at

____________________.

And remember to ask your child to share the learning fun they had on Animal Day!

Sincerely,

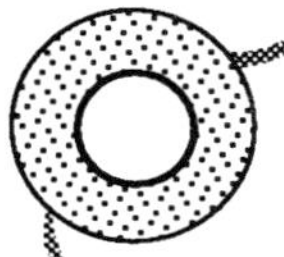

ANIMAL DAY PLAY

THE DAY'S ACTIVITIES

Sit in a large circle. Go around the circle and invite each child to share one special thing about their animal.

Make some animal sounds together. Roar like a lion, chatter like a monkey, trumpet like an elephant. Now you're ready to set off on a a learning safari!

Literature Corner

Cuddle with your stuffed animal while you listen to a story.

Animals Born Alive and Well **by Ruth Heller,** Grosset & Dunlap, 1983
Illustrated and simply presented book about animals and their young.

Who is the Beast? **by Keith Baker**, Harcourt Brace Jovanvich, 1990
Vivid illustrations take a tiger through his jungle explorations as he finds out he is not the only living creature around.

Skill Builder: Sorting

Come together as a group once again with the stuffed animals. Ask the children to make smaller groups according to the color of their stuffed animals. Count how many of each color you have. Now group according to animal. Count the number in each group.

Art Corner

You'll need:

- *tempera paint in several colors*
- *yarn*
- *crepe paper streamers*
- *cardboard box large enough to hold each child's stuffed animal*
- *collage materials*
- *white glue*
- *paint brushes*

Have each child paint their box the color of their choice. When the paint dries, add trim to decorate the box. Turn the box into a float for the stuffed animal. Add a string and pull the animal floats in a parade.

Snack Time

Munch on some animal crackers! Before taking the first bite, take time to develop visual discrimination by looking for matching animals. How many different kinds can they find? Can they name any?

Ready to Rest

Hibernate with your stuffed animals. Say the following chant and name individual children and their animals as they get ready to rest.

"Name of child came to school today,
With his/her pet name of animal who likes to play.
Now they are both tired and ready to sleep,
Quietly they go without making a peep!"

Music

More Piggyback Songs compiled by Jean Warren, Totline Press ,1984 has a selection of songs about animals. The songs are simple and use familiar tunes such as *Twinkle, Twinkle, Little Star*.

Kid in Motion by Greg and Steve, Youngheart Records, has two animal songs. *Animal Action I and II* ask the child to move different ways to mimic a variety of animals.

See Resources, page 7, for details.

Skill Builder: Sizing

Draw an imaginary line down the middle of your classroom. Ask all of the children with large animals to get on one side of the line and those with small to get on the other. Are there more small or large animals?

Next place the animals upon the imaginary line from smallest to largest.

Skill Builder: Oral Language

Ask each child to tell you about their animal. Go into further detail from your opening. Ask questions such as if the animals were real where would it live, would it be big or small or a different color than their stuffed animal. Encourage each child to tell you as much as they can about their animal.

Art Corner

You'll need:

- *tempera paint in a variety of colors*
- *large sheets of butcher paper*
- *paint brushes*
- *paint smocks*
- *masking tape*

Paint a cooperative mural. Tape butcher paper horizontally on the wall for each trio of children. Supply brushes and a colorful variety of paint.

Snack Time

Ask children to bring a color treat such as orange wedges, carrot sticks or yellow cornbread squares to share with a specified number of classmates.

Ready to Rest

Say the following rhyme to settle the children for quiet time.

"Orange, yellow, red and blue,
Lie down if you see these colors on you.
It 's time to take a little rest,
So you will be your very best."

"Pink, purple, green and white,
Lie down and I will turn out the light!
It 's time to take a little rest,
So you will be your very best."

Music

Movin' by Hap Palmer, (see Resources, page 7), is a good choice for the motor development activities that follow. If this recording is not available, instrumental music would be appropriate.

Motor Development

Play music that has different beats, speeds and feelings. Invite the children to move their scarves to the music. Encourage them to use the scarf in one hand, then the other. They can also grasp the scarf with a hand at each end and move their arms simultaneously.

Can they express feeling with their scarf? How would an *angry* scarf move? How would a *happy* scarf move? How would a *tired* scarf move?

Closing

Each child should be holding his or her scarf. Say a color. If that color is in a child's scarf they may wave their scarf through the air while they get ready to leave.

COLOR DAY PLAY

Music

Move to the following songs using paper shapes, small colored items or by finding the colors on their clothing.

Colors by Hap Palmer, from ***Learning Basic Skills Through Music, Volume 1***
Move Around the Color by Hap Palmer from ***Easy Does It.***
Parade of Colors by Hap Palmer from ***Learning Basic Skills through Music, Volume 2.***

Color Walk

Give each child a different color scrap of paper or a small colored item to hold. Take a walk around the school and the immediate area surrounding the school if it is safe to do so. Tell each child to look for things that are the same color as the item they are holding. When you return to the classroom ask each child to share a few of the items they saw.

Skill Builder: Color Identification

You'll need:

- *clear plastic glasses*
- *food coloring*
- *eye dropper*
- *coffee filters*

Fill several glasses with water. Add food coloring to each one. Drop a few drops of varying colors on a coffee filter. Observe the results. Once you have seen several different color combinations begin to mix the different colors of water in the glasses together to get even more combinations. The children can also create designs on the coffee filters.

Motor Development

Have all the children get in a straight line across the room from you. Name a color and a movement that will move them to where you are. "If you are wearing yellow, crawl to me." Continue on with a different color and movement until everyone is beside you. Go to the other side of the room and repeat the game in the other direction.

Skill Builder: Observation

Say a color and ask a child to find something that color in the classroom. They can stand near what they have found until every one has had a turn.

Increase the difficulty and develop oral language by naming following the same procedure but asking a child to describe the item he or she has found. Other children try to guess the item from the clues.

Closing

Ask everyone who is wearing red to tiptoe to get ready to go home. Continue to say a different color and movement until everyone is ready.

Put Your Focus On Your Feet!

GETTING READY:

5 Days before Foot Day, send out the parent information notice provided. One day prior to the event, send home the reminder notice.

You will need these materials for Foot Day Play *Activities:*

Art Corner:
- Tempera paint in various colors
- Wide bristle paint brushes
- Butcher paper
- Bucket of water
- Extra towels

Snack Time:
- Chicken legs
- Electric skillet
- Bread crumbs
- Pie tins
- Cooking oil
- Milk

Skill Builder:
- Four large bins
- Cotton batting
- Shaving cream
- Water
- Extra Towels

Literature Corner and Music:
- See suggested titles in activities

FOOT DAY PLAY

We are planning a special theme day. Please read the information below and gather all the requested items to send with your child on the date indicated below.

Date:_____________________

Please send: A small towel, labeled with your child's name

Other needs:

A reminder will be sent home on the day prior to the special event.

If you would be willing to help, please sign and return this form with your child._______________

FOOT DAY PLAY

Reminder

Tomorrow is our special Foot Day. **Please remember to send** a small towel labeled with your child's name and any other materials requested on our original notice. If you have any questions, please feel free to call me at ___________________.

And remember to ask your child to share the learning fun they had on Foot Day!

Sincerely,

THE DAY'S ACTIVITIES

Opening

Have all the children stand in a circle. Look down at everyone's feet. Compare the kinds and colors of the shoe you see. Take off your shoes and socks. Wiggle your toes. Get ready for a barefoot story time!

Literature Corner

What Neat Feet! **by Hana Machotka**, Scholastic Inc., 1991
A picture of an animal's foot is followed by a picture of the animal and description of how the foot is used. Have children compare their feet to the animals'.

Under Your Feet **by Joanne Ryder**, Four Winds Press, 1990
A poetry book about nature's activities that take place "under your feet".

Hannah's New Boots **by Celia Berridge**, Scholastic Inc., 1992
Hannah has many adventures in her new boots.

Skill Builder: Tactile Awareness

You'll need:

- *four large bins*
- *extra towels*
- *shaving cream*
- *water*
- *cotton batting*
- *extra towels*

Fill each bin with one of the four items listed. Have the children take off their shoes and socks and walk through the different bins. Ask them to describe the textures they feel.

Have an an extra bucket of water and towels handy for feet cleaning and drying. Children should use the towels they brought.

Art Corner

You'll need:

- *butcher paper strip for each child*
- *tempera paint in a variety of colors*
- *wide-bristle paint brush*
- *towel*
- *bucket*

Have children take their shoes and socks off and sit in a chair. Paint the bottom of both feet. Stand children on the butcher paper and let them walk across it. Use the footprint painting for the Skill Builder activity below.

Dip feet in a bucket of water to clean. Dry with a towel.

Skill Builder: Creative Thinking, Language

When the footprint artwork has dried, ask each child to tell you a story about where their footsteps took them and what adventure they had there. Write the story they tell you on the butcher paper.

Snack Time

You'll need:

- *chicken legs*
- *milk*
- *electric skillet*
- *pie tins*
- *bread crumbs*
- *cooking oil*

Give each child a chicken leg. Talk about where the foot would be attached. Have the children compare it to their own leg and foot.

Put bread crumbs and milk into pie tins. Have children dip their chicken legs into the milk then the bread mixture to coat. Have them watch from a safe distance as an adult fries the chicken legs for a tasty snack.

Ready to Rest

When it is time to rest repeat the rhyme and have the children think about ways their feet can move them quietly to rest.

"My feet can hop, my feet stand still,
They take me up and down a hill.
But now my feet can do no more,
They want to rest and hear me snore."

Music

Easy Does It by Hap Palmer (See Resources, page 7) has several songs that deal with different ways feet can move. Listen and move to the music as feet learn to gallop, jump and run, skip, wiggle and hop!

Motor Development

If you do not have the album suggested above, ask children to suggest different ways they can move using their feet.

Try moving in these suggested ways with their shoes on; then have everyone take off their shoes and try the movements once again. Does it feel different without shoes ? Are they able to do the same movements?

Learn a chant to say together while moving your feet.

"My toes how they wiggle,
When you touch them I giggle!
Together my feet can jump and hop,
And if I get tired I'll try to stop!"

Skill Builder: Visual Discrimination

Have all the children take off their shoes and put them in a big pile.

One at a time invite a child go to the pile and find a pair of matching shoes, other than their own.

Skill Builder: Sorting

After children have matched all of the shoes take time to look at them closely. Can they find things that are the same in different pairs of shoes? It might be the color or the way they lace, buckle or zip. There might be boots or slip-ons.

Work cooperatively to sort the pairs into piles with the same features. Some pairs may fit into more that one category.

When finished have everyone find their own shoes and put them back on.

Closing

Have children look at their shoes and their classmates'. Ask them to find a partner that has shoes that have something the same as their own. For example, they tie, have red laces or slip on. Once everyone has found a partner have them tiptoe to the door together. It's time to go home!

All Hands On Deck For Learning Fun!

GETTING READY:

5 Days before Hand Day, send out the parent information notice provided. One day prior to the event, send home the reminder notice.

You will need these materials for Hand Day Play *Activities:*

Opening :
- Extra things worn on or used by hands (polish, rubber gloves, rings, gardening glove)

Art Corner:
- Green & brown tempera paint
- Wide-bristle paint brush
- Construction paper
- Crayons

Snack Time:
- Sugar cookie dough
- Waxed paper
- Baking sheets
- Rolling pins

Literature Corner and Music:
- See suggested titles in activities

Skill Builders:
- Construction paper variety
- Scissors
- Pencil
- Glue Stick
- Marking pens

HAND DAY PLAY

We are planning a special theme day. Please read the information below and gather all the requested items to send with your child on the date indicated below.

Date:____________________

Please send: Something worn on or used by hands

Other needs:

A reminder will be sent home on the day prior to the special event.

If you would be willing to help, please sign and return this form with your child.______________

HAND DAY PLAY

Reminder

Tomorrow is our special Hand Day. **Please remember to send** something worn on or used by hands with your child and any other materials requested on our original notice. If you have any questions, please feel free to call me at __________________.

And remember to ask your child to share the learning fun they had on Hand Day!

Sincerely,

THE DAY'S ACTIVITIES

Opening

Ask each child to bring something that can be worn on or used by a hand. Hopefully you'll get everything from rings to gardening gloves to nail files. You might make some suggestions to parents to help them with their selection. During opening, choose a few for student demonstration. This can be carried on throughout the day.

Literature Corner

My Hands **by Aliki,** Harper Trophy, 1990
Describes the parts of a hand and the many different ways we use our hands and fingers.

Hand, Hand, Fingers, Thumb **by Al Perkins**, Random House, 1969
An easy to read story told in rhyme about the hand, fingers and thumb.

Skill Builder: Directionality

Reinforce directionality by asking the children to put their hands in specific positions.For example:
"Put your hands below your waist."
"Put your hands behind your back."
"Put your hands over your head."

This activity can also be used to reinforce the learning of body parts and listening skills. For example:
"Cover your eyes with your hands then put a hand on each knee."

Increase the number of instructions as sequential success increases.

Art Corner

You'll need:

- *green and brown tempera paint*
- *wide-bristle paint brushes*
- *construction paper*
- *crayons*

Paint the palm side of a child's hand green and the front of their forearm brown. Press the painted hand and arm on art paper. Lift gently. The imprint should look like a tree. When dry, use crayons to add fruit, flowers or other creative detail to the tree. Invite the children to describe their tree to classmates.

Snack Time

You'll need:

- *roll-out sugar cookie dough*
- *waxed paper*
- *baking sheets*
- *rolling pins*

Give each child a large ball of cookie dough to put on a sheet of waxed paper labeled with the child's name.

Show them how to roll the dough flat. Have the children place their hand in the center of the flattened dough and press to make a hand print. Bake the cookies on waxed paper according to recipe or package directions. Serve when cooled.

Ready to Rest

Get ready to rest by playing a quiet hand game. Silently complete an action with your hands and ask the children to follow. Some suggestions are clasping hands together, making a fist, tapping fingers quietly, clapping softly or touching only the thumbs together. Finish by placing the hands together and putting them next to the head. Ask them to lie down and rest for a little while.

HAND DAY PLAY

Music

Hap Palmer has two songs about hands that will enrich the day's activities. (See Resources, page 7, for details.)

High and Low can be found on ***Learning Basic Skills Through Music—Vocabulary***.

Put Your Hands Up in the Air is found on ***Learning Basic Skills Through Music, Volume 1***.

Skill Builder: Small Motor

Here are two finger plays that will increase small motor agility.

My hands move around.
My hands touch the ground.
My fingers can wiggle.
If they touch you, you'll giggle.

My hands can clap.
My hands can slap.
My fingers can snap
and go tap, tap, tap.

Skill Builder: Observation

Increase observation skills with a cooperative study of the hands. Divide into groups of four. Ask group members to lie on their stomachs in a circle on the floor with arms stretched out in front. Their arms are close together. Place palms on the floor. Ask them to tell what is the same and different about each person's hands. Turn the hands over and study the palms. Put hands palm to palm and compare size. What do they observe?

Values

You'll need:

- *construction paper in a variety of colors*
- *scissors*
- *pencil*
- *marking pen*
- *glue stick*

Help each child trace his or hand on construction paper the color of their choice. Cut out the hand. Overlap and glue the hands together into the shape of a friendship wreath.

Write something special about each child on the hands. Ask children to help you think of these special qualities in their classmates.

Motor Development

Teach children a variety of ways they can move that use both hands and feet working together. Try a bear walk, crab walk. Learn a "pair walk" such as the "wheelbarrow". Ask the children to think of some original ones, too. Participate in a wheelbarrow race or relay races involving a variety of these movements.

Closing

When you say a child's name, ask them to move towards the door demonstrating a movement they learned using both of their hands touching the ground!

Save A Sunny Day For Some Shadow Fun

GETTING READY:

5 Days before Shadow Day, send out the parent information notice provided. One day prior to the event, send home the reminder notice.

You will need these materials for Shadow Day Play *Activities:*

Opening :
- Flashlight

Art Corner:
- Flashlight
- Masking tape
- White butcher paper
- Black construction paper
- Scissors
- Black marker

Snack Time:
- Bread
- Peanut Butter
- Jelly or jam
- Napkins
- Plastic knives

Skill Builders:
- Full size mirror

Science
- Colored sidewalk chalk

Literature & Music Corner:
- See suggested titles

SHADOW DAY PLAY

We are planning a special theme day. Please read the information below and gather all the requested items to send with your child on the date indicated below.

Date:____________________

Please send: Flashlight labeled with your child's name

Other needs:

A reminder will be sent home on the day prior to the special event.

If you would be willing to help, please sign and return this form with your child.______________

SHADOW DAY PLAY

Reminder

Tomorrow is our special Shadow Day. **Please remember to send** a flashlight labeled with your child's name and any other materials requested on our original notice. If you have any questions, please feel free to call me at ___________________.

And remember to ask your child to share the learning fun they had on Shadow Day!

Sincerely,

THE DAY'S ACTIVITIES

Opening

Make the room dark. Shine a flashlight on a light-colored wall where the children can move and see their shadows. Regroup after everyone has had a turn. Ask the children what you have created. Can the children find any other shadows in the room?

Literature Corner

Bear Shadow **by Frank Asch**, Simon & Schuster Inc., 1985
Little Bear takes drastic measures to rid himself of his shadow.

My Shadow **by Robert Louis Stevenson,** G.P. Putnam's Sons, 1990
A classic poem about a little boy and his shadow.

Skill Builder: Shapes & Directionality

Go outside for this activity. Let each child find their shadow. Ask them to try to stand behind or in front of their shadow. Once the children realize their shadow moves with them and it is not possible to do these skills on their own, have them find a partner. One child stands still and casts a shadow while the other moves according to your directions. Switch roles half way through the activity.

Art Corner

You'll need:

- *scissors*
- *flashlight*
- *white butcher paper*
- *masking tape*
- *black markers*
- *black construction paper*

Make a silhouette of each child by making the room dark and shining a light on their upper body. Tape white paper on the wall behind the child. This works best if the child is sitting in a chair turned sideways. Trace the silhouette on the white paper. Let the child cut out his or her silhouette and mount it on dark paper.

Snack Time

You'll Need:

- *bread*
- *jam or jelly*
- *napkins*
- *peanut butter*
- *plastic knives*
- *large blanket*

After reading either of the literature selections or talking about how it seems that your shadow sticks to you, make a sandwich of peanut butter and jelly that sticks together the same way that a shadow sticks to something!

Ready to Rest

Invite the children to shadow you with words and actions as you say:

"I ran as fast as I could today,
But everywhere I went, my shadow was there to stay.
I tried to hide but it would not disappear,
It seems no matter where I went, it always was there!
So now I hope if I lie very still,
My shadow will run and hide behind a hill."

SHADOW DAY PLAY

Music

Make the room dark. Listen to *"Gentle Sea, Enter Sunlight, Twilight and Midnight Moon"* from ***Movin'*** by Hap Palmer (see Resources, page 7). Invite children to turn on their flashlights and move the beam of light in time to the music.

Science

You'll need:

- *large supply of sidewalk chalk in various colors*

Go outside early in the day. Let the children pick a partner to help them to trace around their shadow. Each child should write their name on the spot they are standing when their shadow is traced. If time allows, let the children color their shadow with the chalk.

Later in the day, return to your outdoor shadow pictures. Have the children stand on the same spot they did earlier. Trace around the new shadow. Ask the children if they know why their shadow has moved. Briefly explain how the earth and sun move, making the shadow move.

Skill Builder: Directionality

You'll need:

- *full size mirror*

Let each child take a turn in front of the mirror "shadowing" their mirror image. Have them observe the different things their body parts can do.

Ask the children to pick a partner. Facing each other, one child leads the movements while the other pretends to be the shadow. Change roles half way through the activity. Accompany this activity with *"Partners"* from ***Learning Basic Skills Through Music***, Volume 3. (See Resources, page 7.)

Motor Development

Go outside to where you have drawn your shadows. Give the children directions to jump over their shadows using two feet, hop over with one foot, step over the largest part of their body ect. String together more than one direction at a time. Increase the directions by having the children move from one shadow to another. For example: "Jump from your body to another body and touch the nose on that body."

Closing

Darken the room once again. Experiment with your flashlights, making shadows on objects around the room. Then choose one child to be the leader to get the group ready to go home. The rest of the children mirror or shadow the leader to the door.

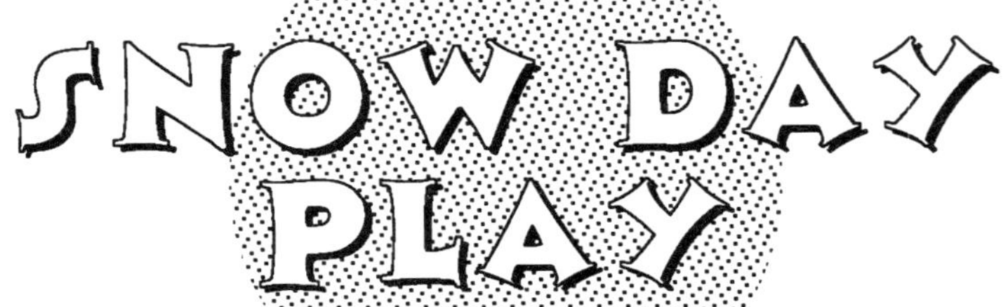

SNOW DAY PLAY

Let Learning Fun Snowball In Your Classroom!

GETTING READY:

5 Days before Snow Day, send out the parent information notice provided. One day prior to the event, send home the reminder notice.

You will need these materials for Snow Day Play *Activities:*

Opening :
- Extra hats or mittens

Art Corner:
- White items:
  paint, chalk, packing pieces
  scrap paper, yarn, cotton balls
- Glue
- Blue construction paper

Snack Time:
- Hot Chocolate Mix
- Marshmallows
- Cups
- Milk
- Pan
- Hot plate

Motor Development; Games
- Ballons
- Paddles
- Ping-pong balls
- Large Nerf Balls

Literature & Music Corner:
- See suggested titles

Skill Builders:
- Bean bags
- Carpet squares
- Food coloring
- Fingerpaint paper
- Bowls
- Plastic hoops
- Ice cube trays

Science

- Ice cubes

- Bowls
- Tub/bucket

SNOW DAY PLAY

We are planning a special theme day. Please read the information below and gather all the requested items to send with your child on the date indicated below.

Date:____________________

Please send: An article of cold-weather clothing labeled with your child's name.

Other needs:

A reminder will be sent home on the day prior to the special event.

If you would be willing to help, please sign and return this form with your child._______________

SNOW DAY PLAY

Reminder

Tomorrow is our special Snow Day. **Please remember to send** an article of cold-weather clothing labeled with your child's name and any other materials requested on our original notice. If you have any questions, please feel free to call me at

____________________.

And remember to ask your child to share the learning fun they had on Snow Day!

Sincerely,

THE DAY'S ACTIVITIES

Opening

Wear something to group time that you wear only when it is cold. Talk about the different items everyone has brought and how they help us to keep warm.

Literature Corner

Thomas' Snowsuit **by Robert Munsch,** Annick Press Ltd. 1985
A funny story about a boy who didn't want to wear his snowsuit.

The First Snowfall **by Anne and Harlow Rockwell**, Scholastic Inc. 1987
A story about changes caused by a snowfall and what to do and eat when it's cold.

The Mitten **by Jan Brett**, GP Putnam's Sons, 1990
A Ukrainian folktale of a lost mitten and animals that take refuge in it.

Skill Builder: Auditory Memory

Place all the clothing the children brought to share with the class in the middle of the group. Give a child the direction to pick two specific items. The child can pick any two that comply with your direction.

Build memory skills by asking the child to try to return the items to their owner. He or she may ask classmates for help or clues.

You'll need a variety of white items:

- *styrofoam packing pieces*
- *white chalk*
- *white glue*
- *white tempera paint*
- *white yarn*
- *blue construction paper*
- *white scratch paper*
- *hole punchers*
- *black construction paper*
- *cotton balls*

Create a winter scene using any or all of the items above.

Snack Time

You'll Need:

- *hot chocolate mix*
- *milk*
- *marshmallows*
- *cups*
- *pan*
- *hot plate or stove*

Make hot chocolate and put a snowball (marshmallow) in each cup. Observe the marshmallow as it melts while you wait for the drink to cool. Caution children against burning their tongue.

Ready to Rest

After some games or a real snowball adventure say this rhyme:

"Snowball fights are lots of work
And make you very cold besides
So let's all find a place to rest
To snuggle up and get warm inside !"

SNOW DAY PLAY

Music

Now that you have talked about bold weather how about freezing your own bodies? Play *The Freeze* from ***We All Live Together Volume 2.*** (See Resources, page 7.) Have the children lie down on the floor and roll around like a snowball when the music goes. When the music stops they FREEZE in place. Movement begins again when the music starts.

Science

You'll need:

- *Tub or bucket*
- *ice cubes*
- *bowls*

Set up a table with a tub of water and bowl of ice cubes. Let children pick up, touch and feel the differences between the two in temperature and texture. Talk about how water freezes.

Skill Builder: Counting

You'll need:

- *several plastic hoops*
- *small carpet pieces*
- *bean bags*
- *large paper numerals*

Have a snowball toss. Set the hoops out around the room. Place a paper number from one to five in the each hoop. Children stand at a area marked by a carpet piece and try to throw as many bean bags into the hoops as the number says.

Motor Development

Dodge the Snowball
You'll Need:
- *large nerf balls*

Form a circle with three children in the middle. The players forming the circle try to hit the children inside the circle with the nerf "snowball". When a child is hit they trade places with the child who threw the snowball.

Snowball Toss
You'll Need:
- *balloons*
- *paddles*

Pair children with a partner. Use a paddle or a "Whammer Bammer." (See resources, ***Make It Today,*** page 6) to hit the "snowball" back and forth .

Skill Builder: Color Recognition

You'll need:
- *bowls of water*
- *fingerpaint paper*
- *ice cube trays*
- *food coloring*

Involve children in mixing and pouring colored water into ice cube trays. Put the trays in a freezer. When frozen, provide paper and let them create a picture with the color cubes of their choice. If weather permits, take the ice cubes outside and create pictures on the pavement.

Closing

Place all the winter clothing near your group time area. As each child retrieves what they brought let them put it on and roll like a snowball before they go home.

PENGUIN DAY PLAY

Waddle Your Way Through Icy Adventures!

GETTING READY:

5 Days before Penguin Day, send out the parent information notice provided. One day prior to the event, send home the reminder notice.

You will need these materials for Penguin Day Play *Activities:*

Opening :
- Extra black or white clothing
- Penguin pictures

Art Corner:
- Black and white:
  Tempera paint, Tissue paper
  Pipe cleaners, Crepe paper
  Construction paper
- Paint brushes
- Scissors
- White glue

Snack Time:
- Vanilla ice cream
- Bowls
- Chocolate sauce
- Spoons
- Whipped cream

Literature Corner and Music:
- See suggested titles in activities

Motor Development
- Scooter boards

Skill Builders:
- Globe
- Large pan of frozen water
- Small items such as blocks
- Black ink pad, crayons, paper

PENGUIN DAY PLAY

We are planning a special theme day. Please read the information below and gather all the requested items to send with your child on the date indicated below.

Date:____________________

Please send: Your child dressed in black and white

Other needs:

A reminder will be sent home on the day prior to the special event.

If you would be willing to help, please sign and return this form with your child.______________

PENGUIN DAY PLAY

Reminder

Tomorrow is our special Penguin Day. **Please remember to send** your child dressed in black and white and any other materials requested on our original notice. If you have any questions, please feel free to call me at

____________________.

And remember to ask your child to share the learning fun they had on Penguin Day!

Sincerely,

PENGUIN DAY PLAY

THE DAY'S ACTIVITIES

Opening

Ask children to come to school dressed in black and white. When you gather for opening group time, ask them what animals the colors black and white remind them of—(zebra, penguin, whale). Tell them they will be penguins for the day. Share pictures of penguins in the Antarctic.

Literature Corner

A Penguin Year **by Susan Bonners**, Delacorte Press, 1981
Illustrated story tells about the life of the Adelie penguins in the Antarctic.

Tacky the Penguin **by Helen Lester**, Houghton Mifflin Company, 1988
Tacky is a penguin who does many funny things and wears funny clothes. This is a good lesson in individuality.

Skill Builder: Science

You'll need

- *large pan of frozen water*
- *small items from classroom such as blocks, crayon, pencil*

Talk about where penguins live and the type of climate they need to survive. Show children the pan filled with ice. Let them try to move the blocks and other small items around on the ice so they can feel the cold the penguins need to survive. Slide the items across the ice then across the desk, carpet and other surfaces. Compare the results.

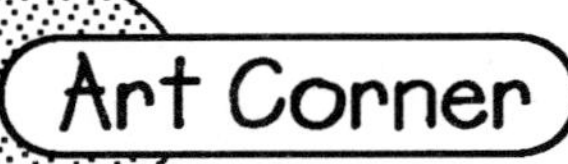

Art Corner

You'll need:

- ***black and white:***
  tissue paper
  construction paper
  crepe paper
  pipe cleaners
  tempera paint
- *paint brushes*
- *scissors*
- *white glue*

Place all of the black and white items and other supplies in the art corner. Encourage individual creativity and let the children make a black and white creation of their choice!

Snack Time

You'll need:

- *vanilla ice cream*
- *chocolate sauce*
- *small bowls or cups*
- *spoons*
- *whipped cream*

Make an icy treat. Scoop some ice cream into a bowl and let the children add their own black and white toppings. Stop eating—if you can—and feel the cold sensation in your mouth.

Ready to Rest

Learn the rhyme then snuggle into your "rookery" for some quiet time.

Today you look like a penguin,
All dressed in black and white.
And now it is time for all to rest,
Get down and out of sight!

PENGUIN DAY PLAY

Music

A cute song about several animal walks that includes a penguin can be found on ***Finger Plays and Foot Plays*** by Rosemary Hallum, Ph.D and Henry "Buzz" Glass. The song is *Penguins*.

Skill Builder: Creative Movement

Play the song suggested above or some other music of your choice and involve the children in some creative movement that develops vocabulary, as well.

Ask the children to *waddle, jump, slip*, slide and *dive* like a penguin. Be sure to have plenty of space so they can move around freely.

You may need to ask for volunteers to demonstrate some moves.

Skill Builder: Number Recognition, Counting

You'll need:

- *black ink pad*
- *crayons*
- *white paper*

Fold the paper into six sections. Write a number from one to six in each section. Ask the children to put as many thumb prints in each section as the number asks for. Use crayons to turn the thumb print into a penguin.

Now practice counting aloud. Hold a number card aloft and work cooperatively to form *rookeries* (penguin living groups) containing that number. Be seated and create a rookery of a different number.

Skill Builder: Social Studies

Ask the children if any know where penguins live. After everyone has had a turn to guess, use a globe to show them where penguins live in relationship to where they live.

Explain that a globe is shaped round like the earth. Talk about the habitat penguins require. Compare it to the children's environment.

Motor Development

Lie down on your stomachs on scooter boards (boards with wheels attached) and pretend to be penguins sliding along the ice.

If you do not have commercial scooter boards, directions for making your own *Sit-Down Scooters* can be found in ***Make It Today for Pre-K Play*** (See Resources, page 6).

If scooter boards are not available, lay a large plastic tarp on the ground and try sliding on your stomachs across the tarp.

Skill Builder: Body Part Identification

Pair the children with a penguin partner and ask them to touch different body parts together. For example, "Put your penguin noses together."

Closing

Ask all the children to who have white shoes or black pants to waddle like a penguin as they gather their belongings. Continue naming other clothing until everyone is ready to leave the Antarctic and waddle for the warmth of home!

Here's Learning Straight From The Heart!

GETTING READY:

5 Days before Heart Day, send out the parent information notice provided. One day prior to the event, send home the reminder notice.

You will need these materials for Heart Day Play *Activities:*

Opening :
- Something to share that is special to you.

Art Corner:
- Red items such as: tempera paint, tissue paper, crepe paper, fingerpaint, sequins, paper scraps, crayons
- Paint brushes
- White glue
- Watercolors
- Markers

Snack Time:
- Red napkins
- Red food such as strawberries, apples, watermelon

Literature Corner and Music:
- See suggested titles

Science
- Stethoscope

Skill Builders:
- Heart puzzles (see directions)
- Flannel board & hearts
- Four paper hearts in four sizes

Motor Development
- Plastic hoops
- Bean bags
- Paper hearts

HEART DAY PLAY

We are planning a special theme day. Please read the information below and gather all the requested items to send with your child on the date indicated below.

Date:______________________

Please send: Your child with something to share that they love. Also try to dress him or her in the color red.
Other needs:

A reminder will be sent home on the day prior to the special event.

If you would be willing to help, please sign and return this form with your child.________________

HEART DAY PLAY

Reminder

Tomorrow is our special Heart Day. **Please remember to send** your child with something to share that they love. Also try to dress him or her in the color red. Please send any other materials requested on our original notice. If you have any questions, please feel free to call me at this

number _____________________.

And remember to ask your child to share the learning fun they had on Heart Day!

Sincerely,

THE DAY'S ACTIVITIES

Opening

Ask each child to bring something they love to school. It can be a picture or the actual item. Give each child the chance to show what they brought. Also ask the children to wear clothing with as much red in it as possible.

Literature Corner

Otto Shares a Hug and a Kiss **by Kathleen Morey,** Kid Love Unlimited, 1983
A rhyming tale of the joy a child receives from a hug and a kiss.

Mama, Do You Love Me? **by Barbara M. Jones,** Chronicle Books, 1991
An Eskimo child finds out that no matter what she does her mother will still love her.

Skill Builder: Visual Discrimination

You'll need:

- *red construction paper*
- *scissors*

Cut out hearts in several different sizes. Cut each heart into two pieces. Be sure the cut on each heart is different. Laminate the heart pieces or cover them with clear plastic contact paper.

Spread all the hearts on a table or the floor. Children may play individually or with a partner to try to "mend the broken hearts" by matching the two pieces together.

You'll need:

- *red colors*
- *tempera paint*
- *crepe paper*
- *glitter*
- *markers*
- *tissue paper*
- *watercolors*
- *fingerpaint*
- *paint brushes*
- *sequins*
- *white glue*
- *paper scraps*

Set all the red items plus the white glue in the art area. Let the children create an original work of art in the color red!

Snack Time

Have a red snack to go along with the red hearts and red clothing of the day. Some suggestions are strawberries, cranberry juice, red apples or tomatoes. Provide red napkins on which to set the snack.

Ready to Rest

Use the hearts made for the matching game to provide a transition to some quiet time. Pass out one half of of a heart to each child. Have the other halves already spaced around the room. When the child finds their matching half they have also found their place to rest.

Game Time

Hide paper hearts around the room. Give the children verbal clues as to where to find them. For example, "Who can find a heart near where we build?" (Hide the heart near the building blocks."

HEART DAY PLAY

Music

Holiday Piggyback Songs compiled by Jean Warren, Warren Publishing House, has several good songs about love, sweethearts and Valentine's Day. See Resources, page 7, for more information.

Skill Builder: Visual Memory

You'll need:

- *four paper hearts, in graduated sizes, for each child*
- *four flannel board hearts, same sizes as children's set*
- *flannel board*

Give each child four paper hearts in graduated sizes. Each child should receive identical hearts. Place the flannel hearts in a pattern on the flannel board. Ask the children to duplicate the pattern they see by arranging their hearts on the floor or table in front of them. For a further challenge take the pattern away and ask the children to recreate it from memory.

Skill Builder: Body Awareness

Give each child a paper heart. Ask the children to follow your verbal directions and touch their heart to different body parts.

"Touch your heart to your ear."
"Touch your heart to your nose."
"Hold your heart over your heart."

Science

Obtain a stethoscope. Give the children an opportunity to wear the stethoscope and listen to the beating of their heart. They may also listen to a classmate's heart. Can they count the beats?

Skill Builder: Shapes

Here's a finger play that will reinforce shapes. Recite the rhyme and draw the shapes with your finger in the air. Invite the children to join in as you repeat the rhyme several times.

I'll draw a circle (Draw a circle.)
And a square. (Draw a square.)
I'll draw a triangle, too. (Draw a triangle.)
I'll draw a heart inside each one. (Draw three hearts in the air.)
A real sweetheart for you!

Motor Development, Counting

You'll need:

- *hoop loops (**Make It Today**, Resources, page 6) or other plastic hoop*
- *bean bags*
- *paper hearts*

Position several hoops in a pattern through which the children can jump. Place a different number of paper hearts beside each hoop. Children move through the hoops, stopping to jump in each one as many times as they count hearts next to it.

Closing

Ask each child to tell their classmates what is so special about the item they chose to bring to share today. This is a good way to be sure they have that "special something" in their possession before leaving!

Make A Learning Splash!

GETTING READY:

5 Days before Water Day, send out the parent information notice provided. One day prior to the event, send home the reminder notice.

You will need these materials for Water Day Play *Activities:*

Opening :
- Pictures of water and water usage

Art Corner:
- Tempera paint
- Wide-bristle paint brushes
- Margarine tubs • Water

Snack Time:
- Fruit juice concentrate
- Pitcher • Spoon
- Paper cups • Popsicle sticks
- Water

Literature Corner and Music:
- See suggested titles in activities

Science
- Two plastic glasses
- Permanent marker

Skill Builders:
- Glass jars in varying sizes
- Metal & wooden spoons
- Plastic hoops • Carpet samples

Motor Development
- Streamers

WATER DAY PLAY

We are planning a special theme day. Please read the information below and gather all the requested items to send with your child on the date indicated below.

Date:______________________

Please send: A picture of water —rain, ocean etc.—or water usage

Other needs:

A reminder will be sent home on the day prior to the special event.

If you would be willing to help, please sign and return this form with your child.________________

WATER DAY PLAY

Reminder

Tomorrow is our special Water Day. **Please remember to send** a picture of water and any other materials requested on our original notice. If you have any questions, please feel free to call me at ____________________.

And remember to ask your child to share the learning fun they had on Water Day!

Sincerely,

WATER DAY PLAY

THE DAY'S ACTIVITIES

Ask the children to bring in pictures of water—from rain to the ocean. One at a time invite them to share their picture.

Literature Corner

Water's Way **by Linda Westberg Peters,** Arcade Publishing, 1991
A simple story tells about the many ways we see water each day.

My Very Best Rainy Day **by P.K. Hallinan,** Ideal's Children's Books,1990
Experience a rainy day with two young children.

Skill Builder: Language

Brainstorm a list together of how the children use water in their lives. Include such things as swimming, taking a bath and watering a lawn.

To prepare children for a pantomime activity, drink a glass of water. Set the glass down and repeat the action in pantomime.

You can also pantomime this rhyme:

Run the water. Take a bath.
Scrubba low and high.
Wrap a towel all around.
Rubba yourself dry.

Now invite the children to choose something from the list to pantomime. Ask classmates to identify the action.

Art Corner

You'll need:

- *tempera paint, slightly diluted*
- *wide-bristle paint brushes*
- *margarine tubs, water*
- *art paper*

Ask children to select the tempera paint color of their choice. Paint the art paper, trying to cover most of the area. Dip a hand into a margarine tub filled with water. Shake your hand and make it rain over the art paper. The paint should still be wet. Children will enjoy seeing the splash marks the water makes.

Snack Time

You'll need:

- *fruit juice concentrate*
- *spoon*
- *pitcher*
- *water*
- *small paper cups*
- *popsicle sticks*

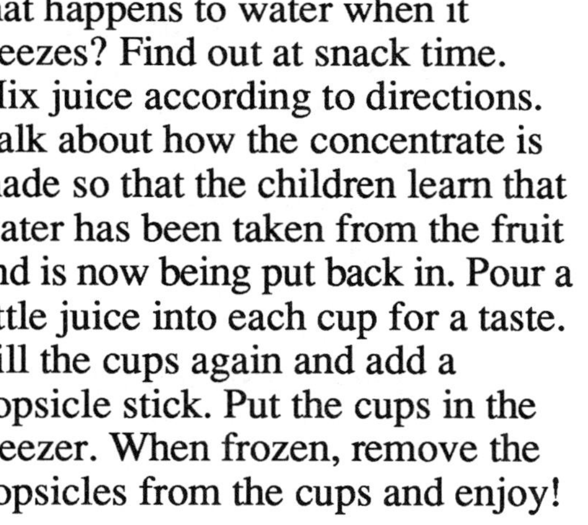

What happens to water when it freezes? Find out at snack time. Mix juice according to directions. Talk about how the concentrate is made so that the children learn that water has been taken from the fruit and is now being put back in. Pour a little juice into each cup for a taste. Fill the cups again and add a popsicle stick. Put the cups in the freezer. When frozen, remove the popsicles from the cups and enjoy!

Ready to Rest

Just before rest time talk about rainy days and how nice it is to be able to snuggle up in bed! Repeat this rhyme.

"Wouldn't you like to snuggle; After you've jumped into a puddle?
In a nice soft bed; With a place to rest your head?"

WATER DAY PLAY

Music

Singable Songs for the Very Young by Raffi, (see Resources, page 7) has several songs about different kinds of water—from the water in a harbor to the water used for brushing teeth.

Environmental tapes that include the sound of rain would also provide a nice background during rest or quiet time, or just for listening. Check with your local music store for an "in stock" recommendation.

Skill Builder: Sound Discrimination

You'll need:

- *several empty, clean glass jars, in varying sizes*
- *wooden spoons*
- *metal spoons*

Fill the jars with different amounts of water. Place them in a line and let the children tap them with the two spoons. Can they hear the difference in the tone? Can they hum and match the musical tones?

Science

You'll need:

- *two identical plastic glasses*
- *permanent marker*

Ask children what they think might happen to water that stays in a glass for a long time. After you get several answers tell them you are going to do an experiment to see find out.

Fill both glasses half way with water. Make a mark on each at the water line. Place one glass inside the classroom and the other outside in a sunny location where it will not be disturbed. Check each glass every day for a week. Mark the new water line if there is a change. Talk about the results at the end of the week.

Skill Builder: Directionality

You'll need:

- *Plastic hoops or Hoop Loops (See **Make It Today**, Resources, page 6.)*
- *carpet samples*

Use hoops and carpet samples to create a "rain puddle" course. Tell the children that each obstacle is a rain puddle. Use directional terms and have them jump *over*, step *beside*, walk *around* and splash *through* the rain puddles.

You can also learn this finger play while waiting for a turn.

Great big raindrops falling down. (Creep fingers down.)
Rain and thunder crashing. (Stamp feet.)
Great big puddles on the ground. (Move hands in circular motion.)
Jump in and let's go splashing. (Jump!)

Motor Development

You'll need:

- *streamers (See **Make It Today**, Resources page 6 or tape crepe paper to paint stirrers)*

Use the music of your choice or any of the instrumental songs from ***Movin'*** by Hap Palmer (See Resources, page 7) and pretend the streamers are "dancing in the rain."

Create thunder showers, rain puddles, raindrops, drizzles and downpours with the streamers.

Closing

Have each child, one by one, pretend to be a fish swimming, a duck splashing or a dolphin diving in water as they move to the door to get ready to go home.

Get Learning Going With Movement!

GETTING READY:

5 Days before Moving Day, send out the parent information notice provided. One day prior to the event, send home the reminder notice.

You will need these materials for Moving Day Play *Activities:*

Opening :
- A few things that "move"

Art Corner:
- Shoebox for each child
- Cardboard circles • Metal brads
- Assortment of tissue, crepe and construction paper
- Yarn or string • Beads
- White glue • Scissors

Snack Time:
- Wheel-shaped macaroni & cheese
- Milk • Butter • Pan
- Spoons • Bowls

Literature Corner and Music:
- See suggested titles in activities

Motor Development
- Scooter boards, tricycles, wagons; play equipment with wheels

MOVING DAY PLAY

We are planning a special theme day. Please read the information below and gather all the requested items to send with your child on the date indicated below.

Date:______________________

Please send: Something that moves (toy truck, pop-up or pull toy)

Other needs:

A reminder will be sent home on the day prior to the special event.

If you would be willing to help please sign and return this form with your child.________________

MOVING DAY PLAY

Reminder

Tomorrow is our special Moving Day. **Please remember to send** something that moves (toy truck, pop-up or pull toy) and any other materials requested on our original notice. If you have any questions, please feel free to call me at ____________________.

And remember to ask your child to share the learning fun they had on Moving Day!

Sincerely,

THE DAY'S ACTIVITIES

Opening

Moving can mean many things to a child from moving to a new city, house, or just simply moving their bodies from one place to another.

Ask children to bring something that moves to school to share during opening. It might be a toy truck, a fan that opens and closes or even a handheld egg beater!

Literature Corner

Up and Down on the Merry-Go-Round **by Bill Martin Jr. and John Archambault,** Henry Holt and Co., 1985 and 1988

Rhyming story describes how a child feels while riding a merry-go-round.

Moving Gives Me a Stomach Ache **by Heather McKend,** Black Press, 1988.

A story about how a boy feels as he leaves the house and friends he loves and starts all over in a new house.

I'm Not Moving Mama! **by Nancy White Carlstom,** Macmillan Publishing Company,1990

A child shares with his mother all of the reasons why he won't move then finally comes to terms with the new adventures he will experience.

It is likely you will have at least one child in the group who has experienced a move from one house, city, state or country to another. After reading one or both of these literature selections, encourage those children to share their stories and feelings about their move.

Skill Builder: Oral Language

Ask the children to name different things that move and tell how they move. Make a list of their ideas. How many of those can you find in your classroom?

You'll need:

- *shoe box for each child*
- *sturdy cardboard circles*
- *scissors*
- *assortment of tissue, crepe and construction paper*
- *white glue*
- *yarn or string*
- *metal brads*

Set out all the materials in an art area. Let the children create a machine "that goes". Use metal brads to attach cardboard circle wheels. Tie on a piece of yarn or string so that the machine will go when pulled.

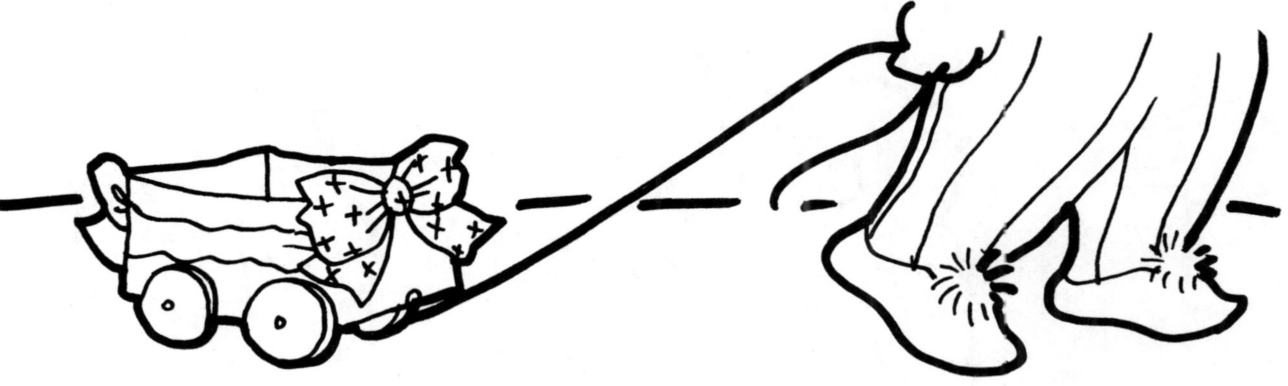

Snack Time

You'll need:

- *wheel-shaped macaroni and cheese mix*
- *milk*
- *spoons*
- *pan, spoons*
- *butter or margarine*
- *small bowls*

Cook some wheel-shaped macaroni and cheese according to package directions. While eating, ask the children to pretend that the wheels are on a train, moving van or car in which they are riding. Where are they going?

Ready to Rest

Ask the children to move like a creeping caterpillar, a slithering snake or a slow-motion snail into a resting position for some quiet time.

MOVING DAY PLAY

Skill Builder: Counting

Say this counting rhyme and do the motions.

One wheel on a wheelbarrow	*(Hold up one finger.)*
Hold the handles so.	*(Hold two hands in front of you.)*
Two wheels on a scooter	*(Hold up two fingers.)*
Make your one foot go.	*(Pedal one foot.)*
Three wheels on a tricycle	*(Hold up three fingers.)*
Pedal round and round.	*(Sit down and pedal with both feet.)*
Four wheels on each roller skate	*(Hold up four fingers.)*
To roll-a-roll around.	*(Pretend to roller skate.)*

Music

Preschool Favorites by Georgiana Liccone Stewart has a number of selections that move the body in many ways, from dancing to bending.

Build auditory memory by asking children to do a sequence of commands such as to touch his nose and then swing his arms. Rub his stomach, touch one knee and then sit down.

Skill Builder: Observation

Take a walk around the neighborhood in which your school is located and talk about the things you see that are moving. Look for running water, a crawling baby, leaves blowing in the wind, cars and bicycles.

Creative Expression

Play music of your choice and let the children move their bodies any way they want to. Be sure to have enough room to move around. Ask the children to share what moving thing they are pretending to be.

Start by naming something to act out such as a flying bird, a floating bubble or a locomotive coming into the station. After a few teacher-created suggestions, ask children to suggest some ideas of their own.

Motor Development

Get moving outside on wheels. Set up a track and have kids follow on anything with wheels—scooters, tricycles, sit-down scooters and wagons. Work with color recognition and meaning, too, by holding up a red or green paper flag to indicate whether to stop or go.

Closing

Shake your knees.
Shake your chin.
Shake your thumbs.
Shake your shins.
Shake your elbows.
Shake your feet.
Shake hands with each friend you meet.

Repeat this movement rhyme, dismissing several children each time until everyone is in line and ready to go home.

More Exciting Titles from **Edupress**

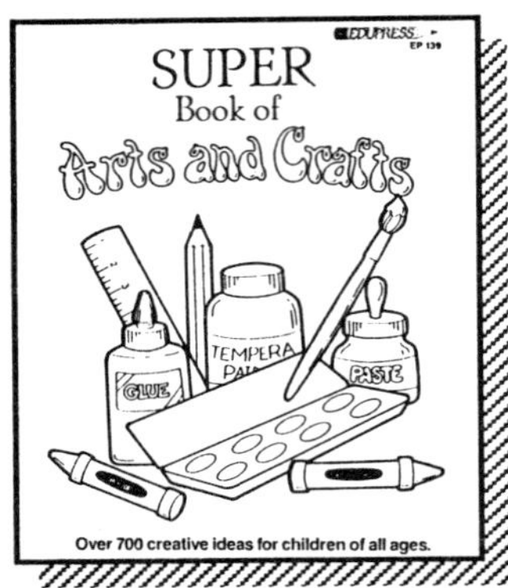

139 **Super Arts & Crafts**
Over 700 art activities

153 **Make It Today**
Easy-to-make equipment

154 **Theme Day Play**
20 Fun-filled days

152 **Easy Games**
Easy-to-make games

130 **Fall Projects**
Multicurricular learning

144 **Literature Patterns**
Interact with literature

145 **Alphabet Patterns**
Hands-on activities

146 **Scissor Skill Patterns**
Cut-and-learn fun

131 **Winter Projects**
Loads of winter activities

123 **Holiday Patterns**
A host of holiday fun

125 **Puppet Patterns**
Multicurricular activities

124 **Poem Patterns**
Link poems & learning

135 **Center Games**
Ten easy game centers

136 **Outdoor Games**
Group and skill games

134 **Holiday Games**
Games for every holiday

111 **Lend An Ear**
Build listening skills